DEHY

COOKBOOK

The Ultimate Beginner's Guide to Dehydrating Food: Including Vegetables, Fruit, Meat & More. 50+ Tasty Recipes

Legal & Disclaimer

The information contained in this book and its contents is not designed to replace or take the place of any form of medical or professional advice; and is not meant to replace the need for independent medical, financial, legal or other professional advice or services, as may be required. The content and information in this book have been provided for educational and entertainment purposes only.

The content and information contained in this book have been compiled from sources deemed reliable, and it is accurate to the best of the Author's knowledge, information, and belief. However, the author cannot guarantee its accuracy and validity and cannot be held liable for any errors and/or omissions. Further, changes are periodically made to this book as and when needed. Where appropriate and/or necessary, you must consult a professional (including but not limited to your doctor, attorney, financial advisor or such other professional advisor) before using any of the suggested remedies, techniques, or information in this book.

Upon using the contents and information contained in this book, you agree to hold harmless the Author from and against any damages, costs, and expenses, including any legal fees potentially resulting from the application of any of the information provided by this book. This disclaimer applies to any loss, damages or injury caused by the use and application, whether directly or indirectly, of any advice or information presented, whether for breach of contract, tort, negligence, personal injury, criminal intent, or under any other cause of action.

You agree to accept all risks of using the information presented inside this book.

You agree that by continuing to read this book, where appropriate and/or necessary, you shall consult a professional (including but not limited to your doctor, attorney, or financial advisor or such other advisor as needed) before using any of the suggested remedies, techniques, or information in this book.

Sommario

INTRODUCTION

With today's seemingly instant food availability and practically every modern home with a refrigerator and food storage freezer, you might ask, "who needs a food dehydrator?" You might say, "If I can get all my fruits, vegetables, meats, etc. to the local grocery store at a moment's notice, why would I ever need a food dehydrator to preserve my food?" But it's a fair question, who needs a dehydrator for food? Lest just talk for a bit about that.

Garden Family

I believe absolutely, without a doubt, that any family of two or more people having any size of a vegetable garden should have a food dehydrator for the kitchen. If, at any time of your life, you have had any experience with a garden, you know the abundance of your harvest is always far greater than your original planting. One tomato plant can be planted to reap a dozen or more tomatoes. The ability of your family to eat all of the harvest abundances in your gardens is probably pretty slim. You have the ability to preserve this product for the enjoyment of your family over the next few months with a food dehydrator. Okay, your neighbors probably won't like you owning this dehydrator because they won't get as many free goodies out of your garden as possible.

Teacher

The average American Student Today has never before been so far removed from the origins of our food supply in our nation's history. A meal dehydrator in the classroom just makes so much sense as a teaching tool. It will offer visual and real-time, hands-on experience for your students with their raw food. For a child to take a strawberry picked from a garden plot in the classroom, dehydrate it and then have it explode with taste in their mouth is a teachable moment that is absolutely priceless. Whether the practical uses of a food dehydrator in the classroom are related to history, science, or home economics, it can be one of the most effective and versatile teaching tools in your classroom.

Outdoorsman

The best friend of the outdoor hunter may be more than merely his trusty hunting dog. The hunter of today needs an additional best friend in the form of an equally trusted food dehydrates. A hunter needs an effective and timely way to conserve the fresh meat after a successful hunting excursion. The gastronomic highlight of the trip can be to turn this meat into a savory, seasoned piece of jerky. One of the most heavily used pieces of camping equipment will be a food dehydrator at the campsite or lodge. When it comes to camping, whether you're a weekend camper, hiker or hardcore survivor, what could be more necessary than a cheap supply of healthy, finger food and snacks to eat on the trail or on the campsite? A food dehydrator will give you that healthy blast of good carbohydrates and proteins your body will crave during these physically challenging events. These dried snacks do not require any preparation or elaborate preservation and are extremely lightweight and easy to pack. Eating these snacks won't require any further food preparation. Literally, dehydrated food can be highly nutritional power snacks that can fit in your backpack or pocket.

Church

Food engineers said food dehydration could be one of the most efficient forms of cost-effective food preservation techniques. This research has been listened to very carefully by churches with a theological belief system based on end-time survival or feeding impoverished world populations. In many families, spiritual and family lives, amassing a home or community storehouse of well-preserved foods using a home food dehydrator is the front and center. Other missionary families recognize a food dehydrator's effectiveness and incorporate it in the feeding of their indigenous followers. These are populations that may suffer due to starvation, natural disaster, or war-torn atrocities due to lack of food. A food dehydrator is recognized as the catalyst that not only satisfies religious needs but also allows one person to effectively feed a multitude of healthy, preserved nutritious food.

So, the question here is. Do you see any of those examples in yourself? Are you in a family of two or more people having a garden of any size? Are you a teacher or a member of a school system looking for creative, inexpensive, and effective teaching tools? Are you a lover of the outdoors who needs a healthy, finger food snack? Are you a member of a church that requires you to keep the food worth at least one year? Does your church support a field missionary who is trying to feed the surrounding people efficiently to spread the message? If, in any of these examples, you see yourself, then you are the one that needs food to dehydrate. Your one-time purchase of a modern home food dehydrator will last for years, from about $50.00 to $250.00. Your food dehydrator will provide you with years of service and quickly become the piece of kitchen equipment you're going to wonder how you've ever been without.

CHAPTER 1

FOOD DEHYDRATORS:

WHY EVERYONE SHOULD HAVE ONE

You might wonder why you'd like to dehydrate your food because it seems they'd take away something from the food instead of adding to it, but that's not really the case. The cycle of dehydration helps the food to retain almost 100 percent of the nutrients. Sometimes as little as 1 percent of the nutritional value is lost, but usually, all vitamin C and fiber are preserved, magnesium and potassium remain untouched, and you'll love the delicious variety of pure flavors. The food would be as nutritious as it was before dehydration, and the cycle also suppresses the growth of microforms such as bacteria, as much as a decade later.

Lengthen Your Foods "Use by" Date

Today's food dehydrators will extract more than 75 percent of the food's moisture and avoid however much moisture the food dries out, allowing you to prolong its "use by" date while preserving its much-needed health benefits at the same time. Through dehydration and preservation of your food in airtight containers, it can last for more than 20 years and, in some cases, more than 30. Imagine exactly how much money you can spare! Now when you see any of your favorite perishable foods on sale, if you own one of today's powerful food dehydrators, you can stock up. If you get used to buying dried food at the supermarket, you know how expensive it can be. You'll be able to preserve all the fresh, nutritious foods at a fraction of the cost when you have a food dehydrator in your home.

Make Your Garden Bounty Last

There couldn't be a handier tool for gardeners to have a vegetable dehydrator in your home then. Why not make your hard-earned bounty last after spending hours planting, then constantly cultivating your homegrown fruits and vegetables? Just make sense to the food dehydrators!

Ideas for Dehydrated Foods

Create a delicious trail mix that mixes dehydrated cranberries, grapes, pineapples, apples and nuts to produce a balanced trail mix that the whole family will enjoy or create high protein jerky out of pork, beef or poultry! Banana chips are another great time favorite expensive in the supermarkets. It is usually recommended that you soak dehydrated foods before consuming them, preferably in distilled water, so that a sufficient amount of water can be absorbed for optimum taste. Also, you can steam dehydrated food that does a fantastic job of plumping it.

In Conclusion

The dehydrator's performance ensures that you and yours will now have edible all the food that would have expired for over a decade. You're going to save money on the food you'd end up throwing away, and with the price of dehydrators lower now than they'd ever been before, there's never been a better time to purchase! Having seen how simple these dehydrators can render food storage, you will never look back.

Many different dehydrators are available for purchase in all sizes. Find one that works for you and start saving money and storing food. The one-time investment is well worth the long-term money you'll save along with the luxury of being able to store food. Having a food dehydrator in the home is no real downside, and it is worth making an investment.

HEALTH BENEFITS OF A FOOD

DEHYDRATOR

There are a few "must-haves" home appliances in your home, such as a toaster, microwave, blender, coffee maker, and a range of other appliances and utensils. Innovations are made every year, and new items reach the market, many worth adding to your collection like today's highly powerful and useful food dehydrator. The food dehydrator has a vast range of uses, including keeping the food fresh (for endless periods of time), potentially turning it into stews in the future, to keeping the dry food sealed for someone who wants to "grab and go" for a quick snack.

While most vitamins are preserved, the nutritional value of dehydrated foods is reduced to some degree, and the mineral content is not reduced. Most vegetable phytochemicals still remain unchanged. Some phytochemicals, lycopene, and polyphenols, are generally more soluble during the dehydration cycle, and a major advantage is that dehydrated foods are also richer in calories and nutrients.

Another advantage of dehydrated foods is that they do not bear the risk of botulism contamination that moist canned foods do; even dried meats are risk-free when processed for the correct period of time at the right temperature.

Food dehydration has many advantages, which range from healthy storage for a prolonged period of time, avoiding spoilage, which retaining even the best taste. Many foods also benefit from being dehydrated, which can make eating them a much more enjoyable experience.

There are different types of food dehydrators out there, and they come in various sizes, styles, and price ranges. Furthermore, most food dehydrators come in three different configurations.

1. Those that blow hot air from an item just below the machine and dehydrate anything that's held in that lower compartment.

2. Those that blast from the top of the system and have easily accessed and opened compartments from above.

3. Last but not least are the food dehydrators that have on their side a heating dock that allows you to stretch the compartment and bring the food in for dehydration.

Operating a Food Dehydrator Usually, you're just turning on the food dehydrator and letting it run its course, but it's important to note that not all dehydrators have the same power levels and not all foods are dehydrated at the same pace. Many models take longer than others, so it's important to ensure that your food gets absolutely dehydrated to last a satisfactorily long time.

Easy to use This is incredibly easy to dehydrate food and is as simple as turning on the "on" switch when the food you dehydrate is in the same compartment as the processing. With your model, you can find the average times online for every food to dehydrate. You may also want to make sure that juicy foods like wet fruits or meat are put correctly in your dehydrator. Many dehydrators will have a food-specific rack on which to put juicier items, and others will not.

One of the best advantages of dehydrated food is that it's so portable; just place it in a plastic container, pop it into your handbag or backpack, and you're good to go. Also, dried fruit is a perfect addition to your morning toast, hot or cold, and you can blend it in with your yogurt or as an alternative to a homemade trail mix. Dehydrated products often require less storage space, so they're the ideal, compact option for holidays and camping trips. In the end, every kitchen should have a food dehydrator inside.

FACTORS TO CONSIDER WHEN BUYING A

FOOD DEHYDRATOR

Dehydrating food is not really rocket science if you think about it. All that a dehydrator really has to do is keep the temperature and the airflow steady. Most dehydrators have a temperature thermostat for maintaining the desired temperature, and a fan for fresh dry air circulation. I highly suggest that you stay away from any dehydrator that does not come with a thermostat and a fan. Since they all hold the temperature and the airflow, almost all dehydrator models take around the same time to dry the same stuff. So when you're shopping for a dehydrated, looking for one that claims to dry food faster than another isn't really fitting. But when determining which dehydrator to purchase, there are other important considerations to consider. The four main factors in determining which dehydration tool to buy are

1. Heat and ambient airflow
2. Access
3. Versatility
4. Materials & quality Two basic designs for dehydrators are available: stackable tray dehydrators; and shelf tray dehydrators.

Each of these two forms of dehydrators has its own specific benefits and disadvantages. Those two prototypes I'll apply to when I analyze each of the factors below.

1. Heat and airflow: Also, heat and air circulation is the most important thing to remember when purchasing a dehydrator. Nothing is more frustrating than watching your batch get drier than another component. Uneven heating and airflow will cause the food, which is closer to the source of heat and air to dry much faster than the food, which is further away.

O Heat and Air Flow-Shelf Tray Dehydrators-In general, the heat and airflow of shelf food dehydrators are quite even due to the simplicity of the system. The trays in a shelf dehydrator slide out and look like the trays in your traditional oven, and they work. In general, this type of food dehydrator has the heating element and fan placed at the back of the device, and the warm air flows uniformly over all trays. Excalibur manufactures the most popular shelf-dehydrators.

O Heat and Air Flow — Economy Stackable Dehydrators — Uneven heat and airflow is a problem that is found almost exclusively in some stackable food dehydrators, especially the less expensive models of department stores. Stackable food dehydrators usually have their heat source placed in the unit's bottom, so the trays on the bottom get the heat and airflow share of the lion. Many model economies don't even have a fan. Owing to the vertical heat and airflow, economic owners of stackable dehydrators have to rotate their trays regularly to prevent over-drying some trays and under-drying others. I recommend you stop stackable dehydrators in the economy.

O Heat and Air Flow — Quality Stackable Dehydrators — New and higher quality stackable food dehydrator models are designed to deliver heat and airflow much more uniformly than cheap versions. I recommend L'Equip and American Harvest / Nesco brand dehydrators for those who prefer the stackable tray dehydrators. The L'Equip and American Harvest dehydrators are constructed in such a way that the fan and heat source are nearly completely sealed off from the trays to avoid unnecessary heat exposure of the bottom trays. The warm, dry air in these dehydrators flows in the middle of each tray through tunnel-like ducts, and is distributed to each tray like the central air system of a home provides cooled air to each room in a building. The L'Equip and American Harvest / Nesco food dehydrators do not need tray rotation.

2. Access: The ease of access to the trays is another consideration to consider when buying a dehydrate. When preparing and setting up the food for dehydration, when monitoring the progress of the food during the drying process, and when you are ready to remove your dehydrated food from the trays for storage, you need to get into the dehydrator trays. It couldn't be easier to set up, check on, and remove food in a shelf dehydrator. -- tray pulls out individually, much as your traditional oven trays do. There's no need to mess with the trays above or below the tray you're working on, with a shelf dehydrator. For stackable dehydrators, the story is completely different. If you want to reach a tray in the center of the stack, all the trays above it must be lifted off. Not only can higher trays be burdensome to carry, but it can also cause unpleasant injuries and spills if the trays topple. Some stackable dehydrators are fitted with 6, 10, 12, or even 20 trays. It's important to remember how the job of so many trays stacked on top of each other can be a little bulky.

3. Versatility: You want it to be as flexible as possible when you are investing in a piece of equipment like a dehydrator. When it comes to usability, each has a different benefit over the other when comparing both the shelf tray dehydrators and the stackable tray dehydrators. First of all, the shelf tray dehydrator has a great advantage when you want to dehydrate "big" items, enabling clearance between trays for times. Much like a traditional oven, you can simply remove trays to get as much vertical clearance as you need between trays. For example, the stackable dehydrator allows you to make dried flowers and beautiful crafts (e.g., dough art, dried apple art, some clay crafts, etc.) that otherwise could not fit between stackable trays in the limited space between. You can also produce yogurt in a shelf dehydrator in your own jars that would not be possible in a stackable dehydrate. While there is not much space between trays between the stackable dehydrators, they do have an advantage that the shelf dehydrators don't have: expandability. Stackable dehydrator models typically come straight out of the box with 4, 6, 8, or 10 trays. However, as your dehydrating needs to expand, you can buy additional trays to improve your dehydrator ability. Stackable dehydrators come with ample heating power and airflow power to extend to at least twice the number of trays they originally carried. On the other side, shelf-dehydrators cannot be extended due to the constraints of their box design. If you're outgrowing your shelf dehydrator, you'll need to buy a whole new unit to increase your drying potential instead of just buying some extra trays.

4. Materials & Price: Eventually, you want it to last when you make a dehydrate purchase. Most of the dehydrators we sell at Meat Processing Products are models of high quality with several year warranties. Most are made of plastic materials certified by the FDA to be durable in food grade. Nonetheless, many people worry about the risk of leaching plastic particles or contaminants into foods at warm temperatures. Although we can't confirm whether this is valid, and the FDA says that these materials are healthy, it's food for thought. Because of this, as well as the fantastic look and apparent durability, many people want to buy an all-stainless steel model dehydrate. Many manufacturers produce Stainless steel shelf dehydrators, like The Sausage Maker and L.E.M. Products for home and commercial use.

FINDING A FOOD DEHYDRATOR FOR

NEWBIES

It should be quick to use a food dehydrating agent. It may, however, feel complicated to food dehydration for newbies. So how do you find the right dehydrator for the food? Decide what to do with this if first. Then decide whether or not you will need 2 dietary dehydrators. This article is still confused well and will fix your food dehydrator buying woes.

Now at the start, I said you need to figure out what you want to do with your food dehydrator. The first answer to the question I expect will be dehydrated food with it, and one of the following should be the second. I will do a lot of dehydration of the food, or I will do a very small amount of dehydration of the food. I suggest a large food dehydrator with about 12-15 trays that can be extended to 24 trays if you want to do a lot, and it should have about 750-1000 watts of power. If you are planning to dehydrate food just to do a small batch all that much, then you may need to downsize a bit and go with a tray power of 500 watts 8-12. The trays are also the circular disk for the record, which is very close to the shelves that you will place in your food dehydrator.

The final step is to determine whether you need one food dehydrator or two? The response to this could be as simple as that below. Are you going to dehydrate meat and fruit/ vegetables in your food? If both of you are going to dehydrate, I suggest that you get two food dehydrators. The reason I'm saying get 2 is that if you need to, you can dehydrate both food types at once. Together, you should not dehydrate meat and fruits / vegetables as the drying times may vary greatly, and one or the other food may end up being dry or worse but not dry enough. That's not to suggest you need 2 large food dehydrators, just buy 2 smaller ones at about the same price as a large dehydrator.

Using the above steps will help you determine which food dehydrator is right for you, and then you will be able to compare various types and sizes of food dehydrators and find the one that is right for what you want to do with them. It'll never be easier to purchase and use food dehydrate.

CHAPTER 2

DEHYDRATION PRINCIPLES

All methods of food preservation operate by slowing down or stopping processes that cause food to spoil, decay, or rot. The wine preserves juice by substituting alcohol for sugar. By converting sugar to lactic acid, brined pickles preserve cucumbers. Freezing food protects it by slowing down enzymatic processes and rendering it too cold for reproductive spoilage species. By destroying spoilage species, deactivating enzymes, and removing oxygen, Canning protects the food. Dehydration works by removing water needed to make enzymes work and ruin living organisms.

Why Foods Rot

Everything produced in the wild comes back to nature. Eventually, the leaves dropping from trees are the soil from which trees draw sustenance to grow new plants. And though food often takes a more circuitous path to its ultimate destination, it is the destiny of all things. Nature guarantees this outcome in the very cell mechanisms.

If a cell is cut off from its food and oxygen sources, as occurs with a steak's cells when a steer is killed, the cell's enzymatic processes don't necessarily cease. Depending on the conditions in which it is processed, such processes will actually continue for many days.

However, the processes are not the ones usually occurring when the animal is alive. Metabolic waste products such as lactic acid and carbon dioxide are eliminated and replaced with fresh glucose and oxygen during a lifetime. This allows for successful cell activity. But the proteins and enzymes inside the cell assume a different character and function as waste products are no longer collected, and new supplies are no longer supplied. In particular, proteins are produced which break down tough tissues and collagen so that microorganisms such as bacteria and microorganisms such as fly larvae can more easily digest the meat.

Although the aging meat cycle is often considered to be a form of rotting, it is not rotting in reality because it does not use spoilage organisms. Rather, aging takes place at temperatures that prevent the rapid growth of bacteria while also allowing the cells' enzymatic afterlife processes to tenderize meat, so it becomes more flavorful. Of course, if the temperature were a little too high or the food stayed unfrozen for too long, the tenderized meat would be a prime meal for microorganisms that would cause short-term rot.

The same is true of fruits and vegetables. For example, the blossom end of the cucumber is cut off while making brined pickles, so that the enzymes do not disperse and soften across the cucumber.

And the first source of spoilage in food is enzymatic. Enzymes within a food product's cells will break it down, soften it, and make it ready for consumption by micro-organisms like fungi and macro-organisms like fly larvae. In addition, these enzymes do not spoil the food, but they make the food susceptible to spoiling organisms and alter their existence.

Microorganisms are yet another source of food spoilage. With the exception of pathogenic diseases, occurring while something is alive and food being traded, microorganisms rarely have much impact. An apple on a tree never spoils, spinach leaves on a plant don't spoil, and bacteria don't harm chickens walking around the yard. It is only when the plant or animal cells no longer obtain new sustenance that they are vulnerable to spoilage, and their waste products are no longer eliminated.

We normally don't eat apples straight off the tree, of course, or pick up a chicken from the yard and eat it completely on the spot with feathers. They are processed, delivered, or harvested, and stored instead. And it is the time that provides the window of vulnerability for microorganisms after harvest or processing.

Microorganisms that are completely harmless to living things get busy with processed and harvested food in a hurry. We create their own populations as they consume the food, and return the nutrients in the food to the earth to repeat the cycle. That's a good thing when this happens in your compost pile. The case is less funny when it occurs on your kitchen counter to organic peaches costing $5/lb.

Microorganisms are not different from other living thing in that to survive; they require those conditions. Some micro-organisms require oxygen, and while oxygen is present, some cannot grow. Many microorganisms grow best at room temperature, and others grow better at temperatures slightly higher or lower. Even, each micro-organism has certain preferred food ranges. Which means they are going to grow in some foods but not in others.

The key factors in food spoilage are these two factors — cellular enzymes and microorganisms —. Other factors may contribute to these processes, and may even be preconditions, but the main is enzymes and micro-organisms.

Sunlight and other bright light sources also play a role in spoilage, because ultraviolet rays can discolor or damage food. Oxidation is yet another cause of damage. You noticed this with the shifting color of a cut potato or an apple. Though the effects made by sunlight and oxidation are not as bad as those made by enzymes and microorganisms, it is important to prevent them in order to make an appealing product.

WHY DEHYDRATION KEEPS FOOD FROM

SPOILING

Water is important to food and to all life processes. There is no water, which means no life. Although this can only be a problem if you have chosen to go hiking through the desert of the Sahara, it is also useful knowledge to preserve food.

Water is the carrier which allows enzymes to work inside cells. If it is removed from the cell, then the enzymes in their tracks are stopped. Most enzymes have a specific temperature range that they function at. Freezing protects food by holding enzymes below their temperature range for activity. Canning protects food by raising the temperature to the point where the enzymes are denatured in such a way that they are broken down and thus can do nothing. Dehydration works by eliminating the water needed for the enzymes to operate. It is crucial to understand that the enzymes may still be (and often are) present in dehydrated foods but are simply inactive due to a lack of water. Enzymatic activity, and consequent deterioration, return once water is added.

Freezing controls, the bacteria by keeping temperatures too low for reproduction. Canning controls bacteria by killing them at temperatures that are high. Dehydration controls bacteria by rendering them uninviting to climate. Microbes need the living and the absorption of water. If conditions are too dry, there are some microbes that form spores and hibernate, but many microbes will dehydrate and die.

An element needn't be dehydrated until it has absolutely zero moisture to protect it. For instance, if you were to dilute a 50/50 ratio of some honey with water, the jar containing the undiluted honey wouldn't spoil, but the diluted honey would. Although it obviously contains some water in the undiluted honey, it does not contain enough water to sustain bacterial growth, although the diluted honey can support bacteria like crazy.

Thus dehydration prevents enzymatic processes and deprives bacteria of the nutrients they need to survive on, thereby avoiding spoilage.

WHAT CAN DEHYDRATE FOODS?

It can dehydrate any vegetable, fruit, meat, or bread. The problem is not so much whether this can be dehydrated as whether it makes sense to do so, or how to use the dehydrated food.

Dehydration is causing significant damage to the structural integrity of food cell walls. As a result, their consistency is not the same as the fresh product when dehydrated foods are reconstituted by adding water. Canned and frozen products are very close to the fresh product, while dehydrated foods are comparatively mushy or soft in most instances. You can dehydrate beef and carrots, but in a soup or stew, the dehydrated items are going to go much better than as a steak main course.

There are some practical considerations, as well. Many foods (such as cauliflower) will have to break their cell walls by blanching to be effectively dehydrated. Other foods like apples can only be dehydrated by cutting, dipping in some lemon juice, and placing them in the dehydrator. Yet other foods, including watermelon, are almost all-water. Watermelon contains so much water that it would take a long time to dehydrate, and all you would have left at the end would be a blurry, pink stain.

So even though, in principle, virtually any food can be dehydrated, you will want to reserve dehydration in practice for foods whose value is enhanced by the process. For starters, dried apples, pears, and bananas make great snack foods; and if you've ever looked at pre-packaged dehydration costs, you're going to know that growing your own dried fruits is definitely worthwhile financially. A tough flank steak which is cut into strips and dried in a stew will be very tender. Dry onion is a rising spice. Until it goes bad, drying baked bread so you can make your own stuffing mix will save you money at Thanksgiving while providing a superior culinary experience compared to mixes.

Of course, it isn't all for dollars and cents. Dehydrated foods can add a convenience dimension too. In the winter, I make plenty of soups so stews, and it's good that I can just reach over and grab a handful of dried carrots, dried celery, dried salsify, or even dried red sweet peppers to add. I powder some dried tomatoes in the blender when I make my own spaghetti sauces instead of using a commercial thickener after it boils down to get the right consistency. They consume the sauce's excess moisture while adding authentic tomato flavor. Drying often concentrates the flavors in food, which is one of the reasons why you use in a sauce so much less dried basil than you would new.

So you can dry foods that you'll find useful in dried form. The spectrum of what might be useful is often not intuitively apparent. Read the recipes on dried salad dressing and soup mixes to get some ideas. While the first ingredient is normally salt, MSG, or some form of starch, you can find onion, garlic, red bell peppers, peas, and similar old friends inevitably afterward. When you see how dehydrated foods are being used, it soon becomes evident that you can produce dehydrated goods that are superior to the ones you can purchase.

Steps to Dehydration The food has four steps to dehydrate: preparation, pretreatment, dehydration, and storage. For a properly preserved product, all four steps are necessary, and the specifics may differ somewhat depending on the specific food.

Preparation involves cleaning or drying, removing seeds or bad spots, and then cutting the food into 1/8"-1/4" slices or strips of uniform thickness.

Methods of pretreatment typically focus on preventing oxidation and breaking down cell walls if required. In the case of meats, it is also important to sanitize the surface by dipping it in a boiling solution.

While dehydration can be practiced theoretically by hanging food in the sun on racks, as is still done in some cultures, you need a dehydrator for the modern schedules. In department stores or over the Internet, you can buy dehydrators, or you can create your own. A fan and the temperature regulation are the main features you want in a dehydrator.

When a plant has been dehydrated, it will have less oxygen than the surrounding air, so by extracting it from the sun, it will begin to replenish the lost moisture. Dehydrated foodstuffs must be kept in airtight containers to avoid this. In most cases, I use wide-mouthed quart canning jars with sealing lids, but I often use sealed vacuum bags or airtight plastic containers. They are stored in a cool, dark spot to prevent sunlight damage.

Preparation

Few if any food is improved in quality through any method of preservation. In fact, the quality of food that isn't fresh will always suffer to a certain extent. So you want to start with the best food that's available. If something is a bit overripe, that's okay, and it's fine to remove any rotten spots as long as you completely remove them. But you also don't want to start off with food that's clearly past its prime. The best-dehydrated vegetables will not be made from flaccid carrots and wilted celery.

You should wash the food you start with to reduce the bacteria. It is enough just to run it underwater in the sink and rub it dry with a paper towel. A lot of people have suffered from food poisoning over the past decade or so as a result of the careless application of raw manure by commercial farmers to crops too close to harvest time. The crops became contaminated with E. Other microbes or coli. Likewise, it is almost impossible to guarantee that raw meat has not been affected by any fecal matter. So wash it off before you start, and blot it dry. If you are processing leafy vegetables, use a salad spinner to dry them appropriately. I picked one for $10, and I love that one.

The food you are going to be dehydrating needs to be cut to properly dehydrate. In general, anything from 1/8 "to 1/4" is appropriate, but it is necessary to have almost the same thickness for all the slices inside a batch. Otherwise, some bits would end up drying way ahead of others.

Uniform slicing is difficult to perform by hand, but on the market, there is a range of inexpensive slicing guides that will give you perfectly uniform slices in no time flat. I picked up the mine for $20 at a large chain pharmacy. It comes with plates for various thicknesses, and it has lasted for many years. These work well for vegetables and fruits, but not for meat. I'll explain how you can make your own slicing guide for meats in the chapter on creating your own dehydrator.

Pretreatment

The pretreatment of fruits and soft vegetables accounts to nothing more than dipping the slices into a solution made of either lemon juice or water-mixed vitamin C. Using 500 mg of vitamin C or two lemon juice spoonsful per pint of water. These act as antioxidants to avoid drastic changes in color from the exposure to oxygen while the food is drying. The fruit is perfectly safe if it is not pretreated with an antioxidant, but it appears more appetizing if it is. For fruits that are cut in half and will take a long time — more than a day — to dehydrate, they are generally either pretreated with a potassium metabisulfite solution (the same stuff used in winemaking) or sulfured by putting the fruits in an enclosed basket over a mound of sulfur placed on it. This is usually used for apricots, peaches, and nectarines. The fumes of sulfur dioxide formed by the burning sulfur combine with water to form an acid that rapidly forms sulfites within the fruit. I use potassium metabisulfite in the form of Campden tablets available from home-brewing suppliers because I do most of my dehydration in the fall and winter when the house is closed, and the smell of burning sulfur is unpleasant. Crush one Campden tablet and one tablet of vitamin C into a quarter of tea.

Their pretreatment consists of steam blanching when dealing with vegetables that have a tougher cell structure. Sources of blanching vegetables include onions, sweet potatoes, carrots, turnips, parsnips, broccoli, cabbage, and salsify. Place them in a boiling steamer for 3–4 minutes to steam blanch your vegetables after they have been washed and cut, then immediately dump them into ice water for another 3–4 minutes. Pat them dry after this, then put them into your dehydrator. Upon blanching, turnips and potatoes will benefit from a dip in the lemon juice to prevent discoloration.

Pretreatment for non-ground meats is achieved by blanching them in boiling water for only a few seconds until the meat surface turns grey. That is enough to kill bacteria on the surface. After icing the meat, there is no need—just place it right in the dehydrator.

Dehydrating

You need a dehydrate to dehydrate. Ideally, you want a configuration with both a fan and power over temperature. For department stores, such as the Nesco®/American Harvest®, the round versions you can purchase typically only have one square foot of space per rack, and they also only have five racks. These are all right for occasional use of small batches, but if you're trying to use them to put away a half-bushel of potatoes or even a tote of apples, you'll quickly find they're not enough for the job. These dehydrators are easy to clean and operate very well and can be found for as little as $35. So if you've got enough space to run 3 at once, you will.

The next level of the dehydrator is something like the fifteen-square-foot-space Excalibur ®, but it bears a pretty heavy $270 price tag. It is still a good option if you plan to do a lot of dehydration if you're not handy and are short on space.

A third option is that of making your own. I describe a big, homemade dehydrate in the final chapter of this book. Depending on how high you make the racks, in a dehydrator, you could have 32 square feet of drying space, which cost around $230 to construct. That's a lot of dehydration for the buck, so if you're good with hand tools and aren't scared by some basic electrical wiring, it's the way to build your own.

Items to be dehydrated are placed without overlapping in a single layer on the racks, temperature control is set, and the device is switched on. Although many dehydrators come with books that suggest a certain period to dehydrate different items, these times are, at best, vague guesses. This is because the drying time can differ with the ambient temperature, the thickness of the bread, the amount of humidity in the food, and the slice evenness. To check if food is being finished, remove a piece of dehydrating and allow it to cool. Vegetables are made when they're rough or crisp. The fruits should be pliable and leathery, but if broken and pinched, they will feel dry and show little moisture. Dry meats and fish should be tough, but rather bendable than brittle. It's all right a little oil showing on meats and fish.

Setting temperature is straightforward. For herbs, spices, and flowers use a temperature between 90 and 100 degrees to preserve their flavors. Similarly, nuts and seeds should be dried between 90 and 100 degrees to prevent their delicate oils from becoming rancid. For the preservation of their vitamin C content, fruits and vegetables should be dried at 130 to 140 degrees, and meats should be dried at 150 to 160 degrees to avoid spoilage during drying.

Storing

Certain of the food in the dehydrator would eventually be done before the rest. Take it out of the dehydrator as food finishes, and store it in an airtight container. Do not mix different foods in the same jar because they are going to transfer the flavors. Keep your containers away from light in a cool spot, and keep them sealed when not in use so that moisture is not absorbed from the atmosphere. Food will keep this way with no problems for up to a year.

If you want to preserve the food for a very long time, use one of the many available vacuum sealers, like the Seal-a-Meall ® or the FoodSaver ®, instead of just using an airtight container. Stored in this way, dehydrated food can keep for four to five years, even at room temperature. If you want to save them any longer, put your sealed vacuum packages at the bottom of a chest freezer where they will stay for about 15 years.

CHAPTER 3

DEHYDRATING FRUITS

Dry fruit is the candy of nature; however, unlike candy, it preserves much of the fruit's intrinsic vitamins, minerals, and fiber, making it more nutritious and satisfying. I stick to a caveman-style diet, and there are candy bars for me, but there are dried fruits (in small quantities). In the fresh fruit, dried fruit retains the minerals, caloric content, and fiber present. They also maintain much of the fresh fruit's niacin, thiamine, vitamin A, and riboflavin. Vitamin C is the only vitamin suffering a substantial loss during dehydration, with fruits losing 90 percent or more of their vitamin C during dehydration. This effect can be marginally ameliorated by pretreating fruit with ascorbic acid before dehydration.

Dried fruit makes a better sweet snack than much of what you can find in the snack section, but dried fruits (other than raisins) that you can purchase in the supermarket appear to be so wild that they are luxury products. As I don't have a chauffeur to drop me off at a Rolls-Royce grocery store, or a personal shopper to take care of it for me, I usually make my own dried fruit at a lower price for a better product.

Dried fruit is a great simple, allowing perfect additions to cereals, fruit and nut mixes, and cake recipes as well. The dried fruits may also be pulverized, combined with hot water, and reconstituted into an applesauce-like consistency. In producing country wines, a little-known use for dried fruit is. When added during the primary fermentation process of country wines, dried fruits contribute sugar, but also offer a distinct and welcome sherry-like quality.

Most of my dried fruit comes back from my apple trees, pear trees, and grapevines, but at the supermarket and farm stands, I do buy bananas, pineapples, peaches, and other fruits. Often, before it goes bad, I buy more than I can use, or I just have a tough week at work, and I'm not home as much as I had planned, and I don't eat as much fruit as I thought. I end up with fruit anyway that will go bad unless I do something about it. Most often, this means taking the dehydrator down.

I have what must be the niftiest invention in the world for apples, although I definitely did not create it myself. It is an apple peeler that will in seconds peel, slice, and cores the fruit. I have a heavy-duty model that has been going on for years. I once used a cheap version, but it broke only a few days after I used it. I end up slicing by hand for other fruits, but even that way, the preparation takes just a few minutes.

Selecting Fruit for Dehydration

Might dehydrate any fruit. The primary question is whether dehydration of that particular fruit would give you the desired end result. Many citrus fruits and some melons have so much water and so little structure of cellulose that dehydration of them results poorly.

Equally significant is the consistency of the starting fruit. Though I've seen numerous recommendations to use only the absolute finest quality fruit, that's not required. For example, I used apples infected with sooty mold (which, after peeling off the skin, does not penetrate under the skin and is unsightly but harmless) to make spectacular dried apples. Dehydration is such a situation that gives a very good way to make use of fruits that would otherwise not be appetizing. Similarly, a perfect candidate for dehydration is the bananas that are slightly beyond the fresh-eating stage and turn brown but otherwise edible. By doing so, you are adding real value.

But the fruit's essential to be strong. I mean by that, it's not something you wouldn't eat new. I will unhesitatingly eat the slightly overripe banana. Then I peeled the apples on the skin then ate them with sooty wax. Still, I wouldn't eat anything that had been rotting, tainted with anything internally, or lost its structural integrity. Because I wouldn't consume those things, I wouldn't either dehydrate them, so dehydration wouldn't make them healthier. You should stop unripe fruit, too. Choosing ripe or slightly overripe fruit is better for dehydration.

Citric Acid/Lemon Juice

Lemon juice can act as a fruit antioxidant, but you need a lot of it as it is combined with 50/50 water to make an efficient pretreatment. Considering the cost of lemons and how long it takes to produce a cup of lemon juice, it's not a really cost-effective choice unless you have a lemon tree, but it's definitely appealing because it's 100 percent fresh. If I dehydrate easily in a small amount, I will just squeeze a lemon into a bowl of water and use that.

Citric acid is the active ingredient in lemon juice, and powdered citric acid can be bought from home-brewing suppliers and also from several major retail websites. It's very cheap; two ounces of citric acid can be purchased for $2.40. (When bought in larger quantities, it is much less costly per unit.) You mix one tablespoon with a quarter of water and pre-treat your fruit by soaking it in the solution for five minutes before putting it on the drying rack. Citric acid is the least expensive fruit pretreatment option, and, among other fruits, it works very well on apples, pears, and bananas. Citric acid is what gives a distinctive taste to lemonade, and you may find the taste more in the fruits you treat with it, but that's not normally a problem. Once fruits are dehydrated, their sugars are absorbed, and it is hard to note the slight amount of acidity imparted by the citric acid that remains on the fruit after it has been washed.

Ascorbic Acid/Vitamin C

Given the crazy prices paid in store for certain vitamin C tablets, you would think it would be cost-prohibitive to use ascorbic acid as a pretreatment, but nothing could be further from the fact. The vitamin C companies pay for fancy stickers, logos, publicity campaigns, etc. But it costs only $3.89 for two ounces (the equivalent of two hundred 500 mg tablets) when you buy vitamin C powder in a small bag from the home-brewing shop!

On the other side, you will use quite a lot of it to make a pretreatment with antioxidants. You need 2-1/2 spoonful's combined with a quarter of tea. High concentrations are required because the heat of the dehydrate is lost. While vitamin C is a more expensive choice for pretreatment, if dehydrated fruit is a big source of vitamin C in your diet, it may be worth considering adding it.

Dehydrating

The actual dehydration is simple, with all the preliminaries of the way. Temperature, airflow, and time are three ingredients.

Water will migrate from a region where it is more concentrated to somewhere where it is less concentrated, on the premise that there is a means for that migration. At higher temperatures, the air can retain more humidity than it does at lower temperatures. For an extreme example, just 17 percent relative humidity at 72 degrees would provide the amount of moisture required to provide a relative humidity of 80 percent at a temperature of 30 degrees. And the colder the air, the quicker and more deeply it can suck moisture out of the food you dehydrate.

Of course, you are attempting to dehydrate the food rather than cook it, so the higher the temperature used, the more adverse the vitamin content — particularly vitamin C — will be affected. Hence the optimum temperatures for dehydration are a solution for achieving the fastest dehydration without cooking and preserving as many vitamins as possible. The ideal temperature to achieve this balance varies with the food being dehydrated, but it is between 120 and 135 degrees for fruits.

Wind stream is required to evacuate dampness loaded air and convey a lower mugginess in the outside air. In present-day dehydrators, this is practiced with a fan with experience, you'll build up an eye for this, yet until your eye is created, here are a few different ways to test whether organic products are sufficiently dry. Take a bit of the natural product, and tear it fifty-fifty. Crush it as hard as possible close to the torn edge. On the off chance that it shows no proof of dampness close to the tear, it is finished. Another sign for most organic products (aside from prunes, dates, and raisins) is that they don't remain together. The last test is to take a few pieces while still hot from the dehydrator and put them in a fixed sack, (for example, a zipper sandwich pack) at that point pop the pack in the cooler. Return an hour and check whether there is a buildup within the pack. In the event that there is, the organic product should be dried longer. On the off chance that there's no buildup, it is finished.; however, it should likewise be possible through a "smokestack impact" on the grounds that tourist is lighter than cold air and will normally rise. So some dehydrators that don't have fans have vents in the base for outside air, and vents in the top for warm air to exit. I would say, fans work all the more rapidly, yet I've had accomplishment with the two structures. Time is the last fixing, and the measure of time required relies on the getting dried out temperature, how thickly the organic product has been cut, the specific natural product being got dried out, and the surrounding moistness. By and by, this can't be anticipated aside from in exceptionally loose terms. It's ideal to just keep the natural products in the dehydrator and beware of it each couple hours until it's finished. Mastermind your readied and pretreated organic product on dryer plate in a solitary layer with none of the edges contacting. This will guarantee exhaustive drying. When the natural product is orchestrated, placed the plate in the dehydrator and turned it on, setting the temperature somewhere in the range of 120 and 135 degrees Fahrenheit. Present-day dehydrators give the two warms by means of an electric warming component and air development through a fan. Since getting dried out was done all through the majority of mankind's history by placing nourishment on racks in the sun, it might appear that cutting edge dehydrators are needless excess; however, this isn't the situation. The achievement of antiquated strategies for getting dried out was directed generally by karma: the encompassing temperatures and mugginess, precipitation, and daylight. Where I live in New Hampshire, mugginess levels throughout the mid-year are only occasionally underneath 80 percent, and there are times where we don't see the sun for over an hour or two during the day, so drying out on racks in the sun will only here and there yield an item that is very much safeguarded and won't shape. In Arizona, conventional strategies work much better. What present-day dehydrators enable you is to make a result of predictable quality reasonable for long haul stockpiling, where the dampness level of the item can be brought well underneath environmental moistness levels in an extremely brief timeframe without form.

When Is It Done?

With experience, you'll build up an eye for this, yet until your eye is created, here are a few different ways to test whether organic products are sufficiently dry. Take a bit of the natural product, and tear it fifty-fifty. Crush it as hard as possible close to the torn edge. On the off chance that it shows no proof of dampness close to the tear, it is finished. Another sign for most organic products (aside from prunes, dates, and raisins) is that they don't remain together. The last test is to take a few pieces while still hot from the dehydrator and put them in a fixed sack, (for example, a zipper sandwich pack) at that point pop the pack in the cooler. Return an hour and check whether there is a buildup within the pack. In the event that there is, the organic product should be dried longer. On the off chance that there's no buildup, it is finished.

Specific Fruits

Pears and apples may be peeled or unpeeled. They'd need to be cleaned and cored. These can then either be quartered or cut in 1/4 "to 3/8" slices after pretreatment and placed on the dryer rack. Citric acid functions well on apples and pears as a pretreatment. I've got a gadget that easily peels apples, cores, and slices, and I highly recommend having one if you're planning to do a lot of apples.

Melons, like cantaloupe, honeydew, and watermelon, can be effectively dehydrated, but due to their high water content, they need to be thickly cut into 1/2 "slices to save something! They do not need pretreatment. Stone fruits, like cherries, prunes, peaches, apricots, and nectarines, need to be washed and pitted.

Conditioning

When your fruit is finished, it must be conditioned before the final storage is completed. Conditioning is a mechanism that allows for the equalization of moisture levels between individual pieces of fruit. In practice, you do this by putting the fruit in an airtight container and allowing it to sit for a day or two while being sealed.

If you find condensation, bring all the fruit back into the dehydrator and try again for a few hours. Otherwise, it is ready for long term storage after the conditioning cycle.

Storage

The gold standard for the preservation of dehydrated fruit is to seal it by vacuum and then place it at 10 degrees or less in a chest freezer. Though I have done this sometimes, it makes the fruit too unpleasant to use. This is, in my opinion, overkill. One of the main benefits of dehydrated foods is that their survival requires no energy, and using energy to preserve it for ten years is overdoing it a little.

Vacuum sealing is certainly worthwhile for fruit that you won't be using long. By evacuating air, you extract all moisture and oxygen from the atmosphere. Oxygen speeds up oxidation, and thus, vacuum sealing improves food longevity. Vacuum sealer bags are comparatively costly and are not always easy to reseal, so they are better used for long-term products to be stored.

In my view, dehydrated fruit is best stored in wide-mouthed canning pots. While the jars admit light and air—both of which accelerate deterioration—as long as the jars are sealed and in a dark position while not in use, there are minimal adverse effects. In fact, the cost savings resulting from years of reuse combined with usability make them ideal for the job.

Reconstituting Dried Fruit

Because of its extreme sweetness, most dried fruits are eaten in this form. There are also situations where it would be beneficial to rehydrate foods, such as crumbled apple added to oatmeal. For general, when mixed with a volume of water approximately equal to the amount of dried fruit, fruits rehydrate sufficiently. Using room temperature water, blend thoroughly with the fruit, and let it sit for 30 to 45 minutes at any spot, stirring occasionally.

CHAPTER 4

DEHYDRATING VEGETABLES

While fruits and jerky are most frequently dehydrated, vegetables should not be ignored. In fact, the majority of my pantry's dehydrated items are made up of different vegetables. While I freeze many vegetables, especially when they are used as a primary course, it is much more convenient to dehydrate vegetables that are used in soups and stews.

Just like much of the body's weight comes from fat, much of the vegetables' weight comes from meat. New, canned, or frozen vegetables take up much less space. It's really easy to use them: just shake a handful out of a jar and restore the lid. Through dehydration and storage, vegetables continue to lose vitamin C while all the other vitamins and minerals they contain remain intact.

Although there are exceptions, most dehydrated vegetables do not go well as a standalone vegetable course with dinner due to the damage to cell walls caused by the dehydration process. This implies you would like a reconstituted vegetable to essentially mimic the fresh product as a blanket guarantee. However, if this lack of similarity does not preclude you from trying vegetables with a unique flavor and texture, you will find that reconstituted vegetables are still perfectly delicious, assuming you began with a good product in the first place.

Another strong use as a nutrient booster for dehydrated vegetables is. When I was a kid, my daughter loved spaghetti but hated vegetables. Then as it was cooking, I would powder dehydrated vegetables in the blender and add them to the spaghetti sauce.

However, in soups, stews, sauces, and dressings, where dehydrated vegetables really shine. You can include, among other ingredients, onion, garlic, red bell pepper, carrots, parsley, lettuce, and celery in the packs of a variety of seasoning mixes for steak and salads. Vegetables add essential savors in and of themselves to the seasoning of sauces and dressings. Beans will soak water for soups and stews while beans cook, and since their cell walls have been weakened during dehydration, they can release their special flavors into the soups and stew more readily than even fresh vegetable will.

Selecting Vegetables for Dehydrating

Although looking at some vegetables, such as broccoli, may seem impossible, any vegetables can be dehydrated with excellent results provided correct procedures are followed. Just like with fruits, while most experts claim you can only use best-of-the-best vegetables, my experience is that as long as a vegetable is fundamentally sound (i.e., not rotten), dehydration will improve it.

A zucchini with a bad spot on it but cannot be sold in its entirety as fresh produce can still be dehydrated after removing the bad spot. You can blanch and dehydrate celery or carrots that have begun to go limp in the refrigerator with excellent results. While some of my dehydrated vegetable stashes come from products brought in from the garden and directly processed, most come from small batches made from things that were going to go bad in the refrigerator.

Preparing Vegetables

Proper vegetable preparation is the key element to success in dehydrating them, and blanching is the main technique. The vegetable cellular structure is much tougher than a fruit structure. Blanching helps soften the walls, so that moisture can be more readily drained from the cells. This also deactivates enzymes that otherwise would predispose to deterioration. Most vegetables benefit from blanching, excluding onions and garlic.

Blanching has two common forms: immersion in boiling water, and steam. Both are equally fine. I tend to favor steam blanching because you lose fewer nutrients from dissolving in the water, and then it's easier to clean because I've got a steaming bath. On the downside, it takes twice as long to blanch steam. The vegetables to be dehydrated should be blanched for two minutes in boiling water or blanched for four minutes with steam.

Once you blanch vegetables to freeze, they go straight into ice water from the blanching pot until they are fully sealed and frozen. But when you blanch vegetables for dehydration, they go straight from the blanching pot onto your dehydrator's drying racks.

Another essential factor in the planning is scale. Until blanching, vegetables should be cut into small, uniform parts, so that they can be easily dehydrated. Vegetables that can be sliced should not be sliced more than 1⁄4 "thick. Vegetables such as broccoli can be cut into chunks no larger than an inch. Unlike fruits that are subject to discoloration and browning, most vegetables are more durable, and pretreatment is not required after blanching. There are a few exceptions, but this does not affect their consistency, onions, salsify, parsnips, PO.

Pretreatment of Vegetables

Unlike fruits that are subject to discoloration and browning, most vegetables are more durable, so that pretreatment after blanching is not required. There are a handful of exceptions. Though it does not affect their consistency, they prefer to brown onions, salsify, parsnips, potatoes, and some squash. If this is to be avoided, pretreatment with either citric acid or a sulfite solution, as stated in the fruit chapter, would be appropriate.

Dehydrating

Dehydration is achieved by placing your cooked and pretreated vegetables in a single layer on dryer trays with none of the edges touching. This will allow for thorough drying. Place the trays in the dehydrator once the vegetables are prepared, and turn it on, setting the temperature between 120 and 135 degrees Fahrenheit. You don't want to use temperatures higher than 135, or the vegetable may "case-harden." This means the vegetable has formed a hard outer crust to prevent moisture from escaping its inner layers, so you're better off on the lower side of that temperature range.

Specific Vegetables

Although the preceding information on vegetable dehydration provides a clear summary, some vegetables have different criteria for the best results.

Beets need to be completely cooked and separated from the skin. Then slice 1/8 "thick and dehydrate. Broccoli and cauliflower should be cut exactly like they should be for serving, with any stems quartered or halved before steam blanching. Brussels sprouts should be cut in half, blanched, then cut-side-down in the dehydrator. Cabbage should have the outer leaves removed then sliced 1/8" thick, as if for sauerkraut, before blanching and dehydration.

Globe Artichokes claim special treatment to deliver a successful product. Slice the heart 1/8 "thick and cook for six minutes in a standard citric acid pretreatment solution before placing it in the dehydrator. Parsley, Okra, Horseradish, and Mushrooms do not need blanching or pretreatment. Onions and garlic do not need pretreatment or blanching, and they will be leathery when completely dry. If you want a less time-consuming way, just bake it in the oven, put it overnight in the refrigerator, then slice it down and dehydrate it the next day. Clean before squeaky. This way, dehydrated potatoes can be powdered in a decent blender and used to make mashed potatoes instantly.

Tomatoes, ripe or white, require neither pretreatment nor blanching. Some people want to strip the skin, and if you want to do that, just dip them in boiling water in a basket before cracks begin to develop, then plunge them into ice water. The skin then falls off with ease. Personally, I am not taking the skin away. Simply slice in uniform slices or short, small wedges, and dehydrate until bordered by leathery and crisp. Powdering dried tomatoes in a good blender makes it easy for the tomatoes to be reconstituted into tomato paste or used as a thickener in sauces or as a base for tomato soup.

Most people advise storing dried tomatoes in olive oil. I explicitly recommend this activity to AGAINST because botulism spoors can withstand dehydration, and dried tomatoes in oil would remove oxygen, providing a perfect environment for botulism toxin production. Commercial operations that render dried tomatoes in oil follow very strict acidification protocols to ensure a pH that is high enough for botulism inhibition. This is not realistic in a kitchen at home.

Storing Dehydrated vegetables

Dehydrated vegetables must be stored in a manner that removes air so that air pollution is not reabsorbed, and they should be stored away from light so that their colors are not bleached. I store my dehydrated vegetables in canned jars with an airtight cover, and away from light in my pantry.

If you plan on holding the vegetables for a long time, using a vacuum sealer to remove all oxygen and secure the food thoroughly will increase its lifespan by at least double. You can store the vacuum-sealed dehydrated vegetables in a freezer if you want to take it to the next level. They should be available for longer than the human lifespan under those conditions.

Rehydration Vegetables

Dehydrated vegetables can be rehydrated by adding boiling water and allowing the mixture to be set. The first thing most beginners lack is the requisite amount of water. Except for greens, which rehydrate with one cup of water per cup of dried greens, all other vegetables require between 2-1/2 and 3 cups of water per cup of dehydrated vegetables.

The second thing newbies underestimate is how long it takes to reabsorb water from the vegetables. While a few vegetables such as spinach, okra, and sweet potatoes rehydrate in around half an hour, it will take about an hour and ninety minutes for most more. When the water has been brought to the boil, stir, cover, and go do something else.

CHAPTER 5

DEHYDRATING MEAT AND FISH

Since dehydration, in a favorable climate, does not require modern technology, for untold centuries, dried meats and fish in various forms have formed the backbone of the diets of many traditional cultures. It is no surprise because protein is important for survival.

Dried fish and meat, usually called "jerky," are where you get the most bang for your buck. The explanation is that most commercial jerky is filled with chemicals and carbohydrates, and if you can find jerky without pesticides, you'll have to sell your firstborn child to buy it. Drying your own meat and fish will provide you with an outstanding supply of jerky for both snacks and instant soups, stews, and on-the-fly stocks.

True jerky is made by slicing thinly all-muscle meat and drying the strips on a dehydrator or in the sun where the environment is favorable. The cut meat can be marinated, grilled, or spiced to soak up flavors.

Some of what in the supermarket is called "jerky" is not made of whole-muscle beef; it is made of inexpensive ground meat. Another explanation for that is an expense, but another is that it is easier to chew dried ground meat. One drawback is that jerky made from ground meat has to be impregnated with nitrites for health reasons. The jury is, in my opinion, still out on nitrites safety1, so this chapter covers making jerky with whole-muscle meats rather than ground meat.

Selecting Meat for Jerky

Nearly every commercial jerky in the U.S. is made from beef, but in principle, nearly any meat can be used to produce jerky. Many types of meat pose a greater risk of parasites and microbes, but with proper planning and processing, these risks can be eliminated. A secondary problem with meats other than beef is that certain meats, especially poultry, are not appetizing unless cooked before dehydration in any way.

Generally speaking, you want the new whole-muscle meat you would usually consume. Whether you normally don't eat ostrich or rabbit or don't like these foods, making them into jerky won't make them appetizing to you anymore.

Meats will come from the farm, from your livestock garden, from hunting, and from many other locations. You ought to be definitely mindful of the potential for fecal defilement of any meat's surface. For the instance of fowl, this is practically likely because of the manner in which they are processed2, yet it can likewise happen with deer that has been gut-shot or something that has been recklessly taken care of.

Parasites, as well, present dangers. Parasite trichinella is mainstream in pork items, just as in bear and raccoon. It was recorded in ground squirrels as of late. Trichinella can be disposed of by freezing meat in partitions no more noteworthy than 6" thick at a temperature underneath 5 degrees Fahrenheit for thirty days. Your commonplace cooler (for example, the one connected to your fridge) can't do this; however, a decent chest cooler can. Twofold check the temperature in the chest cooler with a thermometer and lower it if important. Pursued meat can have a wide assortment of parasites and illnesses. Chatters are very normal and are the hatchlings of a bot fly. These stay simply under the outside of the skin and don't contaminate the meat, so if the meat is cleaned, it is anything but an issue. Tularemia can be an issue with hares and rabbits. Industrially sold bunnies are tried. On the off chance that you are chasing bunnies, use gloves and a veil while cleaning, and if the liver has white or yellow spots, don't eat the hare! Tularemia is adequately perilous to be viewed as an organic fighting operator. The greatest worry with bigger chased herbivores, for example, deer and Rocky Mountain elk, is Chronic Wasting Disease (CWD). CWD is a prion-based illness like "frantic dairy animals" sickness, and if a human is contaminated, it can take a very long time to show. At the point when it does, the subsequent cerebrum harm causes demise. Up until this point, transmission to people has just been exhibited in a test tube. However, given that comparable prion maladies in sheep and dairy cattle can be transmitted to people, and that it can take a long time to give indications in a human, an alert is altogether. On the off chance that you are a tracker, check with your state's down office to check whether you are chasing in a region influenced by the illness. In the event that you are, have the meat tried for CWD, and don't utilize it in the event that it tests positive. Ox-like spongiform encephalopathy (BSE), otherwise called "frantic dairy animals ailment," is an all the more usually realized disease brought about by prions. The prions that cause CWD, BSE, and other spongiform encephalopathies are not, appropriately, "alive." They are atypical proteins that, when brought into the mind, cause different proteins in the cerebrum to crease so as to impersonate them. Infections, parasites, and microscopic organisms would all be able to be devastated by adequate cooking; however, prions can't be crushed by any measure of warmth shy of their all-out burning. That is the reason you shouldn't eat meat that has tried positive for CWD.

Preparing Meat for Jerky

Once the meat has been selected and treated for safety, it should be rinsed in running water and patted dry with paper towels. The meat will cut all the more effectively in the event that you put it in, the cooler for fifteen minutes first. Cut back any noticeable excess, and afterward cut in strips among ⅛" and ¼" thick. Any length is fine. With red meat, it is normally simple to see the grain of the meat, and in the event that you cut opposite to the grain, the jerky will be simpler to gnaw off and bite. In spite of the fact that any really sharp blade will work, you'll have the best outcomes with a clay blade and plastic cutting board. By and by, I utilize a pleasant carbon-steel edge newly honed.

Dehydrating

Arrange the cooked and marinated strips of meat in a single layer on dryer trays, with no edges touching. This will allow for thorough drying. Put the trays in the dehydrator once the strips are prepared, and turn it on, setting the temperature between 145 and 165 degrees Fahrenheit. If you haven't marinated the meat, remain on the lower end of the temperature range; but use temperatures no lower than 145 degrees Fahrenheit in either case because it's crucial that the meat reaches temperatures that will destroy pathogens throughout.

Jerky marinades appear to be rather fragrant, and at the same time, can affect the taste of everything else dried, so jerky should be the only element in the dehydrate.

How long it takes to produce jerky depends on the initial amount of moisture in the beef, the drying temperature, ambient moisture, and other factors. Meat should be kept in the dehydrator until it's hard to bend (but still bendable), and when you bend, you see distinct cracks.

Conditioning

Like berries, the jerky has sufficient residual moisture to be conditioned before final storage. Conditioning is a method that enables the amount of moisture between different pieces of jerky to be equalized. You do this by placing the jerky in an airtight jar and making it sit for a day or two while being sealed.

When you detect condensation, bring all the jerky back into the dehydrator and try again for a few hours. Meat normally includes a little bit of fat that may have volatilized during dehydration, so test whether any condensation you find is water or grease. If it is grease, don't think about it (as shown by its slipperiness between the fingers). Otherwise, bring it back in the dehydrator and then repeat the conditioning cycle for a while. Your jerky's ready for long-term storage after the conditioning cycle.

Storage

The most reliable way of preserving jerky is to seal it by vacuum and then position it at 10 degrees or less in a chest freezer. Jerky preserved in this fashion will keep you safe, but in my opinion, it's overkill.

Sure, vacuum sealing is perfect for jerky that you don't want to use early. By evacuating air, you extract all moisture and oxygen from the atmosphere. Oxygen speeds up oxidation, and thus vacuum sealing improves food longevity. Vacuum sealer bags are comparatively costly and are not always easy to reseal, so they are better used for long-term products to be stored.

In my view, in wide-mouthed canning jars, the best way to store jerky intended for use over the next few months is. Although the jars admit light and air — both of which accelerate deterioration — as long as the jars are sealed and in a dark position while not in use, there are minimal adverse effects.

CHAPTER 6

DEHYDRATING BREAD

You've used dehydrated bread if you've ever used a prepackaged stuffing mix, bread crumbs, or croutons. Such products are very costly, and often contain ingredients that you would rather not have (such as oils to make spices stick to). Dehydration of bread is easy enough, but dehydration of cake, pita bread, and other baked goods can go far beyond basic bread.

Selecting Bread for dehydration

Although any bread can be dehydrated, if the proportion of oils (especially vegetable oils) in it is minimal, the resulting product will keep better. This is because vegetable oils when combined with anything else and left at room temperature for a time, are highly susceptible to developing off-flavors and strange smells. When using commercial bread loaves, read the label and make sure that the fat content is below 2 g. To serve.

It's even better if you can use a bread machine to make your own bread, so you can control the ingredients when you make your own bread. Whether you replace coconut oil or palm kernel oil with butter when making bread intended for dehydration using a bread machine, the preservation qualities of the final product will be greatly enhanced due to the consistency of those oils.

The advantage of using a bread machine is that the spices (such as sage and rosemary for fowl stuffing) can be mixed directly into the bread. In this fashion, you can avoid making spices stick to the dried bread, depending on added oils. You already have hundreds of recipes in the manual, if you have a bread machine. You can find lots of information in my book, The Mini Farming Guide to Fermenting, if you want to know more about baking bread, both using bread machines and using conventional sourdough methods.

Cake may also be dehydrated, but just as oils make a difference with bread longevity, they make a difference with cake too. For this reason, it's easier to make cakes for dehydrating purposes. The only commercial cake I find suitable for dehydration is angel food cake.

Storing Dehydrated bread and cakes

Dehydrated bread and cakes are fragile and can quickly turn into crumbs if they are not properly packed and stored. These tend not to shrink too much when drying, as opposed to other dehydrated products, and they may also be very bulky. Wide-mouthed mason jars fit well as for most dehydrated items, but you'll want to use the quarter size. Another way is to use vacuum sealer containers, catch as much air as you can within them and seal them without evacuating the gas. This turns the bags into protective balloons. If you were to evacuate the food, the bread or cake would be pulverized by the exterior heat.

CHAPTER 7

DEHYDRATING HERBS AND SPICES

Many exotic spices, including cinnamon, nutmeg, and cloves, can't be grown in the Northeastern United States without a prohibitively expensive artificial climate. But a host of herbs that are commonly used for spicing or herbal tea are fast to grow. This includes, among other things, mints, basil, oregano, tarragon, rosemary, chamomile, anise, borage, caraway, dill, thyme, cilantro, fennel, lovage, herb, and savory season.

I have two beds on my mini-farm dedicated to growing herbs. I do so because certain herbs, such as lemon verbena, are best used fresh, but also because growing and drying for culinary use of my own herbs and teas save a lot of money. Just a few ounces of dried basil or tarragon cost a lot at my local supermarket. Since I like to use a lot of herbs in my meals, growing my own herbs and drying them adds to my bottom line. The quality of the herbs that you cultivate and dry yourself is typically higher, moreover. Yet the fact that I can cultivate herbs like savory and lemon balm, which practically unavailable at the grocery store, is even more important.

Selecting Herbs for Dehydrating

With this, the most important rule is the same as the most important rule about what you would grow in a garden, or what vegetables you can dehydrate: just grow and dehydrate the herbs you really want. Experimenting with stuff that you have never done before makes sense, just in case you want it. But if you don't like basil, it is a waste of time dehydrating a bunch of it.

Generally speaking, you want herbs to be harvested during their most vigorous growth, and before they set seed so that they are sweeter. When you pick them early in the morning before the sun volatilizes the essential oils they have stored throughout the night, you can also get more flavor.

Preparing Herbs for Dehydrating

Regardless of the countless birds flying over and mice roaming about, herbs need to be washed thoroughly before drying. When picked, herbs should be well-washed in cool running water, then gently dried in a spinner for salad. The use of freshwater helps protect natural oils. Salad spinners are available in large department stores for $15 or less.

Using a pair of sharp scissors to cut off the stem from the desired portion of the plant. This will usually be leaves, but it will be flowers in the case of other plants, such as chamomile. Simply cut the desired portion of the plant off the stem, but don't remove any more leaves or flowers.

Dehydrating Herbs

The active herbal principles are generally, but not always, essential oils which can be easily pushed away by excess heat. Even with herbs, whose flavor is primarily a result of non-volatile elements, excess heat sometimes contributes to bitterness. The herbs should also be dried at temperatures that do not exceed 115 degrees Fahrenheit. Place herbs in the dehydrator on a fine-meshed sheet, and leave until they become crisp.

Storing Herbs

Even though the herbal bottles you can find in the grocery store are usually finely chopped or dried, that's the last thing you want to do to a herb until the very minute it's used. Herbs should be kept as pure as possible for storage purposes. The explanation is that chopping or grinding the dried herb exposes much more surface area, which at the same time allows more of the flavoring compounds to escape, thus reducing the flavor of the remaining components through oxidation.

So the desired herbal parts should be stored in a manner that is as intact as possible.

Herbs are better sliced, dried, or powdered right before use. You will see a tremendous difference if you have ever compared freshly milled pepper from a pepper mill to that from a can in the grocery store. The same is true for every herb or spice.

Being fragile, the dried herbs should be stored for protection in a rigid jar. Vacuum sealing is not practical, because it will convert dried herbs into powder. You do want to store herbs to give as little space as possible for oxygen. So I consider using the smallest available canning jars, which are usually 8 ounces or 1/2 pint jars. Sunlight ravages plants, so keep them hidden from the sun. Heat can cause unnecessary flavor changes as well as the loss of flavor components, so store them in a cool place as well.

CHAPTER 8

RECIPES

Chicken Jerky

INGREDIENTS:

1 1/2 pounds boneless skinless chicken breast tenders, sliced into strips about 1/4 to 1/8 of an inch thick

1/2 cup low-sodium soy sauce

1 teaspoon lemon juice

1/2 teaspoon garlic powder

1/4 teaspoon black pepper

1/4 teaspoon ground ginger

Directions: Mix all the ingredients except the chicken in a gallon-sized ziplock bag. Attach the strips of chicken, seal the bag, and make sure all of the meat is covered with marinade. Place the bag in the refrigerator for about 20 minutes.

Place the meat strips on dehydrator trays. Dry for 5-7 hours at 145 degrees, or until completely dry (length of drying time depends on strip thickness).

Quick Bread - Banana Nut

INGREDIENTS

2 big Eggs

1/3 cup Vegetable oil

3 1/4 cup "Fast Bread Mix" show rapid bread mix

1 cup banana chips

INSTRUCTIONS

Preheat oven to 325 degrees Fahrenheit.

Pour the 'Fast Bread Mix' pre-made into a large mixing bowl.

Enable the dehydrated banana chips to soak for 10 minutes in 3/4 cup hot water.

Mix all the ingredients into the bread mixture and add 1 cup of freshwater.

Load into a sprayed 9x5 loaf pan with cooking oil.

Bake for 50 minutes, at 325 degrees.

Quick Bread- Apple Raisin

INGREDIENTS

1/2 cup Cut nuts

2 Large Eggs

3 1/4 cups Fast, Bread Mix,

1/3 cup Vegetable oil

1/2 cup white grapes

1/2 cup Dehydrated apples

1 1/4 cup Water

Directions

Preheat oven to 325 degrees.

Pour the 'Fast Bread Mix' pre-made into a large mixing bowl.

Mix all ingredients in the bread mixture, then add 1 1/4 cup of cool water.

Load into a sprayed 9x5 loaf pan with cooking oil.

Bake for 50 minutes, at 325 degrees.

Scalloped Potatoes

INGREDIENTS

3 tbsp Flour

2 cup Milk

1 cup Cubed ham optional

1/2 cup Dehydrated sliced onion Can replace chopped scallions with dehydrated.

6 Cups Sliced potato dehydrated Scalloped Potatoes

INSTRUCTIONS

Preheat oven to 350 degrees Fahrenheit.

Allow potatoes to soak for 20 minutes in 4 cups of boiling water, then put them in a tub.

Mix together the flour, milk, and dehydrated onions, then pour over the potatoes in the casserole pan.

Cover and bake in the oven for 45 min at 350 degrees. Uncover and bake for another 15 minutes.

Strawberry Coconut Crackers

INGREDIENTS

1/2 cup Coconut juice or water

1/2 cup Shredded fresh coconut or unsweetened coconut

1 cup Ripe hulled strawberries

2 tbsp Strawberry coconut juice

INSTRUCTIONS

Preheat the dehydrator to 125 ° F. Place on a dehydrator tray a drying pad.

In a blender, put the ingredients and combine until smooth.

Verse the mixture of the cracker on the drying board.

Take the dehydrator tray and smack a few times to level it on the table.

Place the mixture onto the drying sheet in a 10-inch square, smooth the surface with a spatula of rubber and use a straight edge to get nice edges.

For 6 hours, dehydrate.

Remove the tray from the dehydrator and cut the square into 2-inch square crackers using a pizza wheel or a straight edge.

Place the tray back for another 6 hours in the dehydrator.

Snap them apart from the perforated lines when the crackers have finally cooled.

Vegan Split Pea Soup

INGREDIENTS

1/2 tsp dry thyme

1/2 tsp Dry basil

1 1/2 tsp Salt

1 tsp Parsley flakes

1 tsp Dehydrated sliced garlic cloves

1 tbsp Vegetable oil or olive oil

1 whole bay leaf

1/3 cup Dehydrated carrots

1/3 cup Dehydrated celery

1/3 cup Dehydrated onion

1/2 cup Dishy barley

1 cup Dehydrated potato

2 cups Split peas

1/2 tsp Black pepper

12 cups Water

INSTRUCTION

Stir in all ingredients.

Remove well, rising heat to simmer and stir occasionally.

When the potatoes and barley are tender, remove, and serve from oil.

I chose this recipe to add pre-made meals to my long-term food storage because it's vegan, and it doesn't include meat.

Though, if you happen to have ham, bacon, or spam, for the meat-eaters. Just throw it in!!

Storing Soups Long Term

INGREDIENTS

1 oxygen packaging

1 vacuum bag

1 Mylar bag

1 ziplock bag Storing soups Long-term

INSTRUCTIONS

Packaging soup Put all dehydrated soup ingredients or stew them into a vacuum bag excluding beef, bullion cubes, starches, flour, or condensed milk.

Place the cubes of bullion, starch, flour, or powdered milk in a zip-lock (or other) container, then put them in your vacuum bag.

Note, long-term stocking of your own dehydrated meats is not recommended. Do not include these in the kit.

Add one bag of 100cc oxygen, then seal with a vacuum.

Etiquette your bag and put it in a Mylar bag to stop glare. That will guarantee the longest shelf-life.

If you want to put more than one soup per Mylar bag, cover each vacuum bag in plastic wrap so that no holes are created by potential rubbing together.

Mark contents and date of your Mylar bag.

Your soup will last for 30 years if properly stored!

To prepare soup, simply open the bag and pour it into the crockpot with the amount of water required. Add the cubes of bullion, starch, ect too.

Care to take the oxygen mask away!

Now is the time if desired to add the fresh meat.

Let cook slow and enjoy!

Sweet Potatoes Bake

INGREDIENTS

6 Cups Dehydrated sliced sweet potato

1/2 cup Brown sugar

1 quarter Orange juice

2 tbsp Cinnamon

2 tbsp Nutmeg

1 stick butter (1/2 cup)

INSTRUCTIONS

Preheat oven to 350 degrees F.

Boil 3 cups of water with sweet potatoes, brown sugar, orange juice, cinnamon, nutmeg, and butter until thoroughly combined and mashed.

Place in a casserole tin, suitable for the oven.

Cover saucepan and bake at 350 degrees for 50 minutes.

Uncover and bake to the brown top for an extra 10 minutes.

Fruit Bread

INGREDIENTS

1 cup Dehydrated sliced dates

7 cups Unseasoned flour

1/2 cup Margarine

1/2 cup Wheat germ

1/2 cup Ground cloves

1 tbsp Anise seed

1 tsp Cinnamon

1 tsp Salt

1/4 cup Brown sugar

1 cup Apple juice

2 tbsp Active dry yeast

4 cups Assorted dehydrated fruits

1/2 cup Chopped walnuts

1/2 cup Chopped almonds

INSTRUCTIONS

Break the fruits into 1/4 inch parts.

Heat the apple juice just below the boiling point and then add the cut fruits and set aside for rehydration.

Soften the yeast in 1/2 cup of warm water (110 degrees) in a bowl or bread mixer for 5 minutes.

Add 1 1/2 tablespoon of warm water, butter, brown sugar, salt, anise, cloves, cinnamon, wheat germ, and margarine melted.

Gradually add 3 1/2 cups of flour and mix for 5 minutes at medium pressure.

Add 1 1/2 tbsp of flour. To knead by machine, add the flour until the consistency is right.

Knead over for five minutes.

Take from the mixer, put it in a greased bowl, switch to grease top, cover and let it rise until doubled (1 1/2 hours).

To the fruit, the mixture adds the dates and nuts.

Position half the dough on a lightly floured surface. Flatten to a circle about 1/2 inch wide.

Position half of the fruit mixture on top and work over the dough slowly, adding just enough flour to keep it from sticking.

Let the remaining dough flatten and repeat.

Place in two well-greased 5 x 9-inch loaf pans, cover lightly and let rise until doubled (1 hour) in a warm spot.

Brush the loaves with melted butter and bake in a 350-degree oven until the bread pulls away (about 1 hour) from the sides of the plate. If it's browning too fast, cover lightly with foil.

Remove from the pans, and allow the racks to cool.

Quick Bread Mix

INGREDIENTS

1/2 tsp ground cloves

1/2 tsp Allspice

3 tbsp ground cinnamon

5 tsp Baking soda

5 tsp Baking soda

1 cup Powdered milk

1 1/2 cups Brown sugar

8 cups Flour

1/2 tsp ground ginger

2 tsp Salt Fast Bread Mix

INSTRUCTIONS

Mix the dry ingredients together in a wide mixing bowl and blend for several minutes.

Place 3 1/4 cups of mixture into 4 different vacuum bags (each bag makes one loaf).

Put in one pack of 100 cc oxygen, vacuum seal, and date (good for about 5 years if properly packaged).

Apple Oven Pancake

INGREDIENTS

2 cup Dehydrated apples

1/2 cup Dehydrated green grapes

3 tbsp Butter

4 large Eggs

1 cup Sugar

1/2 tsp Cinnamon

1/4 cup Brown sugar

2/3 cup Flour Apple Oven Pancake

INSTRUCTIONS

Combine the dehydrated apples and grapes together, then add 1 cup of boiling water and allow to soak for 15 minutes.

Place the pie plate in an oven that is preheated to 350 °.

Bake for 15 minutes and then cut.

Place the potatoes, sugar, rice, and 1 tbsp butter in a mixing pot.

Remove from the oven and sprinkle with powder sugar. Pour this mixture over the ingredients in the pie plate that was removed from the oven. Change the temperature to 425 and put the pie plate back in the oven for 15-20 min. Dehydrated raspberries garnish with.

Split hot and drink. This is really cool too.

Granola Bars

Crushed sunflower seeds

1/2 cup crushed cashews

1/2 cup crushed walnuts

1/2 cup crushed peanuts

2 2/3 cup Oatmeal

4 tbsp Butter

2 tsp Vanilla extract

1/2 tsp Sea salt

2 cups Dried fruit

INSTRUCTION

Preheat oven to 400 degrees.

Mix nuts and oats properly, then place the sides in a baking tray.

Toast in the oven, stirring every 3-4 minutes for 10 minutes.

Combine the oil, brown sugar, butter, vanilla extract, and salt in a saucepan, stirring continuously and boil.

Both ingredients, like dried fruit, are thoroughly combined in a large pot.

Dump the granola mixture onto a piece of wax paper, baking sheet, plastic cutting board, or.

Compress and distribute the paste equally so that when you break them, the bars won't fall apart.

Let them dry for about 3 hours on the counter.

I cut mine into bars and placed it in a 115 degree dehydrate.

Package or bubble wrap.

Hash Brown Omelet

INGREDIENTS

2 cups Dehydrated hash browns

1/2 cup Dehydrated chopped onion

1/2 cup Dehydrated chopped green pepper

1 cup Diced ham or brushed sausage

6 whole Eggs

1/4 cup Milk

1/4 tsp Black pepper

1/4 tsp Salt

1/2 cup shredded cheddar cheese

INSTRUCTIONS

Mix carrots, onion, and green pepper in a dish.

Cover with boiling water, then allow to rehydrate for 10 minutes.

Saute carrots, onion, and green pepper in butter until tender in 10-inch non-stick skillet. Sprinkle on ham.

Beat eggs, sugar, pepper, and salt in a bowl; add to the bath.

Lift edges as the eggs attach, allowing an uncooked portion to float below. Remove from heat when eggs are set.

Sprinkle with cheddar cheese, put in half the omelet.

Cover before the cheese is melted for 1-2 minutes.

Beef Barley Soup

INGREDIENTS

1/2 cup Dehydrated cut or diced

1/4 cup carrots Dehydrated onion

1/4 cup Dehydrated barley

4 cups Cooked beef

2 big bouillon cubes

1 whole dehydrated bay leaf

INSTRUCTION

Put both ingredients in a 6 cup water crockpot.

Cook slowly at maximum for 5-6 hours.

Season with salt and pepper.

See the 'Storing Soups Long Term' recycle for the long-term market.

Chicken Dumpling Stew

INGREDIENTS

3/4 tsp Rosemary

1/2 tsp Tarragon

1/4 cup Dehydrated chopped scallions or 1/4 cup diced onions Dehydrated chopped celery

1/2 cup Dehydrated cubed potatoes Using 1 cup of dehydrated sliced potatoes.

1/2 cup Dehydrated diced bell pepper Blend of red, orange, purple

1/2 cup Dehydrated carrots

1/2 cup Dehydrated peas

1/2 cup Dehydrated mushrooms

1/4 cup Powdered milk

2/3 cup Flour

4 Chicken breast halves coated

2 big chicken bouillon cubes

2 cups Bisquick or other baking blend Chicken Dumpling Stew

INSTRUCTIONS

In crockpot, blend flour and powdered milk in 10 cups water until I

Remove remaining ingredients, except for the Bisquick.

Place the cover on and cook for 5 1/2 hours at maximum.

Mix 2 cups of Bisquick with 1 cup of water in a small pot, then swirl.

Apply the Bisquick blend one heaping tablespoon at a time, about 1/2 hour until you're ready to serve. These will cook in big dumplings with biscuits.

Vegetable Soup With Ginger

INGREDIENTS

1/2 cup Dehydrated julienned zucchini

1/2 cup Dehydrated cubed potato

1 cup Dehydrated sliced tomatoes

2 tsp ground dehydrated ginger

1/2 tsp Dehydrated garlic

1/2 cup Dehydrated sliced bell pepper

1/4 cup Dehydrated diced celery

1/2 cup Dehydrated sliced onion

1 cup Dehydrated corn

1 tsp Paprika

1 tsp Crushed basil

INSTRUCTIONS

Position both ingredients

See 'Storing Long Term Soups' compost for long-term storage.

Barley and Collard Green Soup

INGREDIENTS

4 whole Dehydrated collard green leaves

3 whole Vegetable bouillon cubes

1/2 cup Pearled barley

1/4 cup Dehydrated scallions

1/2 tsp Nutmeg

6 cups Water

INSTRUCTIONS

Put the ingredients in a crockpot with 6 cups of water.

Cook for about 4 hours at high.

See the 'Storing Soups Long Term' recycle for the long-term market.

Chocolate Walnut Brownies

INGREDITIONS

4 oz. Chopped unsweetened chocolate

1/2 cup Chocolate flavored shortening

2 cups Sugar

2 tsp Vanilla extract

4 tbsp Powdered whole eggs

1 cup Flour White or whole wheat

1 cup Chopped walnuts May cover pecans

4 tbsp Coffee

INSTRUCTIONS

In a bowl on the burner, over very low heat, melt chocolate and shorten, mixing continuously until smooth. Completely Awesome.

Preheat oven to 350 ° C.

Remove the sugar and cinnamon, then stir well until mixed.

The powdered eggs and 4 Tbsp water are combined in a separate shallow bowl.

Attach the egg mixture to the pot, and start stirring.

Add the flour and nuts to the saucepan and stir until mixed.

Pour the batter into an 8x8 inch grated pan.

Bake for 25 minutes, or vacuum before a toothpick comes out.

Deep Dish Apple Pie

INGREDIENTS

1 tbsp Apple powder

3 tbsp Corn starch

5-6 cups Dehydrated sliced apples

1 cup Sugar

1 entire pie crust Pre-made frozen or home-baked Deep Dish Apple Pie

INSTRUCTIONS

Put dehydrated apples in a big bowl and fill with adequate boiling water to cover the apples fully.

Let apples sit for 5-10 minutes, then drain water off.

While the apples are still sweet, add the remaining ingredients and mix.

Prepare your pie crust while the mixture cools.

Bring the pie together and pour filling in.

Sprinkle over the crust with a little cinnamon and butter.

Place in preheated oven for 40 minutes at 350 degrees.

Papaya Pineapple Coconut Gelatin

INGREDIENTS

1 package orange gelatin

1/4 cup Dehydrated cooked papaya

1/4 cup Dehydrated cooked pineapple

1/4 cup Dehydrated coconut crushed papaya pineapple cocoon

INSTRUCTIONS

Add 2 cups of hot water to the orange gelatin mix.

Apply papaya, pineapple, and coconut to hot Jell-O and require to cool and rehydrate fruit to stand at room temperature for 20 minutes.

Place in the fridge and chill until strong.

TIP: Note you have to use cooked pineapple and papaya, which have been dehydrated afterward. Fresh papaya contains an enzyme that breaks down gelatin, which does not fix the gelatin.

Peach Crumble

INGREDIENTS

2 cups boiling water

4 cups Dehydrated peach slices

1/2 cup whole wheat or white flour

1 cup Packed brown sugar

1 tsp Cinnamon

1/2 cup shortening butter

1/2 cup Chopped almonds

INSTRUCTIONS

Preheat oven to 375 degrees Celsius.

Boil the water in a saucepan.

Layer the dehydrated peaches in an 8 x 8 baking platter.

Pour boiling water on the peaches, and allow the topping to stay until mixing. Let them sit for 10 minutes.

Combine the remaining ingredients in a separate bowl with a large fork until crumbly.

Sprinkle the peaches uniformly over the edges.

Tap the baking dish for the crumbs to settle.

Bake for 45-55 minutes or to brown before white.

Strawberry Banana Smoothie

INGREDIENTS

2 cups Milk

1/4 cup Dehydrated strawberries

1/4 cup Dehydrated sliced bananas

5 Ice cubes

1/4 cup Yogurt

3 tsp Sugar

INSTRUCTIONS

Blend together the milk, bananas, and strawberries and put in the refrigerator for 15 minutes.

So long as it is equivalent to 3/4 cups of dehydrated fruit, you can shift the fruit to some other dehydrated fruit (except citrus).

Handmade Yogurt

INGREDIENTS

1 tablespoon Date sugar or dehydrated crushed coconut or wheat germ (for garnish)

1/2 cup Dehydrated fruit of choice

1 tbsp Yogurt

1/2 cup Powdered milk

4 cups Fat-free milk Homemade yogurt

INSTRUCTIONS

Attach powdered milk to liquid milk and mix it in the saucepan.

Bring to simmer.

Upon having a boil, let it cool off to about 120 degrees F. (This is a really important step).

In a separate small container: add some milk to a heaping yogurt table cubicle and stir.

Mix the tiny bottle back into the big original jar.

Load the milk / yogurt mixture into four small mason jars (approx. 1 cup) and screw onto the lids.

Remove all racks, except the bottom rack, from the dehydrator, and place the mason jars on the rack.

Dehydrator set to 115 degrees F. (Warm the dryer before use).

Dehydrate for about 6 hours, or until the yogurt-like consistency of your product is firm.

Refrigerate the bottles overnight, until the yogurt is solid.

Fold softly in any dehydrated fruit you want to add to your yogurt, then placed back in the fridge for 1-2 hours.

Garnish with date sugar (dehydrate for 15 hours with freshly sliced dates, then grind to a fine powder), dehydrated coconut, wheat germ, etc.

Baked Potato

INGREDIENTS

1 entire Russet baking potato

1 tsp Olive oil

1/2 tsp Salt

INSTRUCTIONS Prepare potato by washing and poking full (no spot left unpunctured) of holes with a fork (both top and bottom) to ensure the holes penetrate into the potato heart.

Rinse potatoes and allow dry air before dried fur. Coat the entire potato with an olive oil film and then salt the skin outside.

Place potato on the top oven rack (with a pan under it on the bottom rack to trap starch dripping) then let potato bake at 325 for 50 min. Break potato top with a knife in a star shape.

Let bake until fluffy and crisp, for another 20 minutes.

Let the potato cool down and cut in 9-10 smaller bits. Place in a dehydrator and require to dehydrate until fully hard during the night.

REHYDRATE: Soak bits for 30 to 40 min in a cup of hot water or before tender.

Pasta Primavera

1/2 cup Dehydrated chopped onion

1/2 cup Dehydrated broccoli

1/4 cup Dehydrated sliced carrots

1 cup Dehydrated sliced sweet peppers

2 tbsp Olive oil

1 cup Dehydrated sliced mushrooms

2 tsp Dehydrated basil

1 tsp Red pepper flakes

1/4 cup Whole wheat flour

1/2 cup Powdered milk

2 tsp Dehydrated parsley

1 tsp Salt 8 oz Linguine

1 cup Parmesan cheese

INSTRUCTION

In another bath, rehydrate broccoli, carrots, and peppers, with 3 cups of boiling water. Set aside for 20 minutes until the remaining water is drained then hydrated.

Sauté the onions and garlic in oil for 1 minute in a large pot over high heat.

Remove chips of broccoli, peppered cabbage, mushrooms, basil, and red pepper.

Switch to medium heat.

Remove rice, then sprinkle with salt and pepper.

Mix fresh milk, dried sour cream, and 1 cup of warm water in a bowl with a whisk until it is creamy.

To thicken, add the bowl to the bath.

Consistency right by applying water to make a smooth sauce.

Bring salted water to a boil in yet another bowl. Add the linguine, then drain and serve al dente.

Pour the combination of vegetables over the linguine and scatter with the parmesan cheese and parsley.

Red Beans and Rice

INGREDIENTS

16 oz Bag of small red beans

14 cups Water

1/2 cup Dehydrated chopped onion

1/2 cup Dehydrated chopped celery

1/4 cup Dehydrated chopped green pepper

1 tbsp Dehydrated parsley

2 whole Bay leaves

1 tbsp Dehydrated garlic, crushed

2 tbsp Olive oil 1 tsp Black pepper

1 tbsp Salt

1 tbsp Worcestershire sauce

1 tbsp Tabasco sauce

4 cups cooked rice

INSTRUCTIONS

Drain the beans three hours before dinner and then placed back into the pot.

Stir in the onions, celery, green pepper, parsley, leaves of the bay and garlic.

Add water to cover the contents: Water for about 4 cups.

Bring to a boil, then transition to medium heat and uncover for 2 hours to simmer.

Add more water if need be. Then, add the oil, pepper, salt, Worcestershire sauce, and Tabasco sauce, if using.

Switch down the heat to nil, cover the pot, and start cooking for 1 hour.

Serve over rice, which is fried.

Pork Fried Rice

INGREDIENTS

1/4 cup Dehydrated carrots

1/4 cup Dehydrated peas

1/4 cup Dehydrated chopped onion

2 tbsp Powdered whole eggs

1 can Remove from pork chunks

1 can be fried rice seasoning

4 cups cooked rice

2 tbsp Soy sauce

1/2 tsp Salt

1/2 tsp Black pepper

1 cup Water

INSTRUCTIONS

Rehydrate carrots, peas, and onions by putting in 1 cup of boiling water and letting sit for 20 minutes

Blend together 2 tbsp of dried eggs and 2 tbsp of water.

Heat oil in a wok or saucepan and whisk in pork, browning lightly.

Attach the pork to the egg mixture and scramble well.

Fill the wok with seasoning mixture, rice, and soy sauce and stir well.

Add carrots, peas, and onions and keep frying for another 3 minutes or until vegetables are tender.

Macaroni and Cheese

INGREDIENTS

6 cups Water

1 tsp Salt

2 cups Macaroni

2 tbsp Powdered milk

1 cup Powdered cheese

INSTRUCTION

Boil water in a saucepan and add salt.

Remove the macaroni and cook until then drain almost tender.

Mix in 1/4 cup warm water with dry milk.

Mix with 1/2 cup warm water and dehydrated cheese powder.

Place the macaroni back into the bowl and add milk and cheese.

Stir thoroughly to mélange. If it feels too thick, add a little more milk.

Chicken Salad Sandwich

INGREDIENTS

15 oz cans chicken chunks

1/2 cup mayonnaise

2 tbsp Dehydrated chopped celery

1 tsp Chopped onion

2 cups Dehydrated bean sprouts

INSTRUCTIONS

Mix all ingredients together.

Let set on sandwiches for 15-20 minutes before spreading out.

Assemble and enjoy sandwiches.

Sweet Potatoes Bake

INGREDIENTS

6 Cups Dehydrated sliced sweet potato

1/2 cup Brown sugar

1 quarter Orange juice

2 tbsp Cinnamon

2 tbsp Nutmeg

1 stick butter (1/2 cup)

INSTRUCTIONS

Preheat oven to 350 degrees F.

Boil 3 cups of water with sweet potatoes, brown sugar, orange juice, cinnamon, nutmeg, and butter until thoroughly combined and mashed.

Place in a casserole tin, suitable for the oven.

Cover saucepan and bake at 350 degrees for 50 minutes.

Uncover and bake to the brown top for an extra 10 minutes.

Brussels Sprout Slaw

INGREDIENTS

2/3 cup Brussels shredded dehydrated sprouts

1/4 cup Dehydrated chopped scallions can replace green onions.

1/4 cup Dehydrated seedless white and purple grapes

1/4 cup Dehydrated halved apricots

Cut 1/4 cup Dehydrated shredded bell pepper

1 whole Dehydrated cherry pepper Crumbled

1/2 cup White vinegar

1/2 cup sliced almonds

1 cup Water

INSTRUCTIONS

Use 32 ounces Mason Jar, mix in Brussels sprouts, green onions, raisins, apricots, and red bell pepper.

In a saucepan, place the vinegar, sugar, cherry pepper, and water and bring it to a boil.

Empty the boiling mixture into the mason jar over the ingredients, then allow it to cool to room temperature.

Fill the jar with extra warm water to top.

Place the lid on top, and cool for 48 hours.

Remove excess from the fridge and drain away. In a bowl, pour and insert into the sliced almonds. Serve, and have fun!

Watermelon Taffy (Dehydrated Watermelon)

INGREDIENTS

2/3 cup Dehydrated shredded Brussels sprouts

1/4 cup Dehydrated chopped scallions Can substitute green onions.

1/4 cup Dehydrated seedless white and purple grapes

1/4 cup Dehydrated halved apricots Chopped

1/4 cup Dehydrated shredded bell pepper

1 whole Dehydrated cherry pepper Crumbled

1/2 cup White vinegar

1/2 cup Sugar

1/2 cup sliced almonds

1 cup Water

INSTRUCTIONS

Using a 32 ounce Mason Jar, layer in the Brussels sprouts, green onions, grapes, apricots, and red bell pepper.

Place the vinegar, sugar, cherry pepper and water in a saucepan and bring to a boil.

Pour boiling mixture over ingredients in the mason jar, then let cool to room temperature.

Fill the jar to the top with additional warm water.

Place lid on top and refrigerate for 48 hours. Remove from refrigerator and drain off excess. Pour into a bowl and fold in the sliced almonds. Serve and enjoy!

Brussels Sprout Slaw

INGREDIENTS

2/3 cup Dehydrated Brussels shredded sprouts

1/4 cup Dehydrated chopped scallions Will replace green onions.

1/4 cup Dehydrated seedless white and purple grapes

1/4 cup Dehydrated halved apricots Cut

1/4 cup Dehydrated shredded bell pepper

1 whole Dehydrated cherry pepper Crumbled

1/2 cup White vinegar

1/2 cup sliced almonds

1 cup Water

INSTRUCTIONS

Use 32 ounces Mason Jar, mix in Brussels sprouts, green onions, raisins, apricots, and red bell pepper.

In a saucepan, place the vinegar, sugar, cherry pepper, and water and bring it to a boil.

Pour the boiling mixture into the mason jar over the ingredients, then enable it to cool to room temperature.

Fill the container with extra warm water to top.

Place the lid on top, and cool for 48 hours.

Remove waste from the fridge and drain away. In a bowl, pour and insert into the sliced almonds. Serve, and have fun!

Apple Crisp

INGREDIENTS

5 cups Dehydrated apples

1 1/2 cups Brown

3/4 cup sugar Butter

1 1/2 cups Flour

INSTRUCTIONS

Soak 5 cups of dehydrated apples in 6 cups of boiling water (about 15 minutes or until hydrated). Do not use excess water to wash.

Load into the baking pan, which is 9x12.

Take brown sugar, flour, and butter, then cut and scatter over the end.

Bake for about 40 minutes, at 350 degrees.

Broccoli Rice

INGREDIENTS

3 cups White rice Brown rice takes longer to cook

7 cups Water

1 cup Dehydrated broccoli

INSTRUCTIONS

Apply 6 cups of rice and water to a rice cooker.

Layer dehydrated broccoli and 1 cup of boiling water into a separate pot.

Enable broccoli to sit up for a couple of minutes until partially rehydrated.

Attach the broccoli to the rice cooker, close the lid, and cook according to desired consistency.

Apple Oven Pancake

INGREDIENTS

2 cup Dehydrated apples

1/2 cup Dehydrated green grapes

3 tbsp Butter

4 large Eggs

1 cup Milk

1/2 tsp Cinnamon

1/4 cup Brown sugar

2/3 cup Flour Apple Oven Pancake

INSTRUCTIONS

Mix the dehydrated apples and grapes together, then add 1 cup of boiling water and allow to soak for 15 minutes.

Place the pie plate in an oven that is preheated to 350 °.

Bake for 15 minutes and then cut.

Mix the eggs, milk, rice, and 1 tbsp butter in a mixing bowl.

Remove from the oven and sprinkle with powder sugar. Pour this mixture over the ingredients in the pie plate that was removed from the oven. Change the oven to 425 and put the pie plate back in the oven for 15-20 min. Dehydrated raspberries garnish with.

Cut hot and drink. This is really cold too.

Black Bean Soup

INGREDIENTS

1/2 cup Dehydrated asparagus

1/2 cup Dehydrated corn

1/4 cup diced bell pepper red or yellow

1/2 cup diced tomatoes may substitute a 16 oz.

May cut 1/2 cup tomatoes

Dehydrated 32 oz diced onion.

Canned black beans

2 whole 4 cups Chicken bouillon cubes Food

INSTRUCTIONS Add onions, peppers, asparagus, yellow squash, tomatoes, bouillon cubes of corn and chicken to four cups of water in a crockpot.

Spray with spices.

Simmer on low at crockpot for 5-7 hours.

Applesauce

INGREDIENTS

4 tbsp Apple powder (Dehydrate cooked apples, and then grind in a blender or food processor)

1/2 cup Hot water

INSTRUCTIONS

Mix water and apple 'stuff' and let sit.

Using 2 part water to 1 part powder to generate whatever amount you need.

Beef Barley Soup

INGREDIENTS

1/2 cup Dehydrated cut or sliced

1/4 cup carrots Dehydrated onion

1/4 cup Dehydrated barley

4 cups Cooked beef

2 big bouillon cubes

1 whole dehydrated bay leaf

INSTRUCTIONS

Put all ingredients in a 6 cup water crockpot.

Cook slowly at maximum for 5-6 hours.

Season with salt and pepper.

See the 'Storing Soups Long Term' recycle for the long-term market.

Baby Food

INGREDIENTS

1 tbsp Powdered

1/4 cup squash Water

INSTRUCTIONS

Dehydrate cooked squash (in this case, butterfly), then run under a blender to make flour.

You can not get a texture even: it may vary from fine to coarse.

In a bowl, add the squash and water and blend.

Microwave, then run again for 20-30 seconds.

It can be served alone, or starter cereals can be added. Should not use honey in children less than 1-year-old to sweeten.

Barley and Collard Green Soup

INGREDIENTS

4 whole Dehydrated collard green leaves

3 whole Vegetable bouillon cubes

1/2 cup Pearled barley

1/4 cup Dehydrated scallions

1/2 tsp Nutmeg

6 cups Hot water

INSTRUCTIONS

Put the ingredients in a crockpot with 6 cups of water.

Cook for about 4 hours at high.

See the 'Storing Soups Long Term' recycle for the long-term market.

Baked Potato

INGREDIENTS

1 whole Russet baking potato

1 tsp Olive oil

1/2 tsp Salt

INSTRUCTIONS

Prepare potato by washing and poking full (no spot left unpunctured) of holes with a fork (both top and bottom) to ensure that holes penetrate into the potato heart.

Rinse potatoes and allow dry air before dry skin. Coat the entire potato with an olive oil film and then salt the skin outside.

Place potato on the top oven rack (with a pan under it on the bottom rack to catch starch dripping) then let potato bake at 325 for 50 min. Break potato top with a knife in a star pattern.

Let bake until fluffy and crisp, for another 20 minutes.

Let the potato cool down and break in 9-10 smaller bits. Place in a dehydrator and allow to dehydrate until fully hard during the night.

TO REHYDRATE: Soak bits in a cup of hot water for 30 to 40 minutes or again until they are tender.

Dried vegetable seasoning powder

INGREDIENTS

16-gram Dehydrated tomatoes

6-gram Dehydrated celery

3-gram Dehydrated mushrooms

2 gram Dehydrated sliced sweet peppers

2-gram Dehydrated chopped onion

2-gram Dehydrated carrots

1 gram Rosemary

1 gram Oregano

1 gram Dehydrated spinach

1 gram Dehydrated bok choy

1 gram Dehydrated summer squash

1 gram Dehydrated beets

1 gram Dehydrated kale powder

1 gram Dehydrated kale

Switch to a tiny glass jar, like a food jar for children, and keep it in your cupboard.

Usage Ideas: For an MSG-free veggie or chip dip, apply a tablespoon of this powder plus 1/4 tsp salt to 1/2 cups sour cream.

For a fast and flavorful soup, add 2 tsp to a quarter of chicken broth (also add shredded carrots and spaghetti noodles, if you wish).

During the morning, I add a slice of a scrambled egg.

When you brown chicken for frying, I add a tbsp to the flour.

Chicken Couscous

INGREDIENTS

1 tbsp Olive oil

1 tsp Dehydrated Garlic Crushed

1 cup Dehydrated tomatoes Cut or split

30 oz Canned chicken with juice

1 cup Water

2 whole chicken bouillon cubes

1/2 cup Raisins

1 1/2 cup Couscous

2 tbsp Dehydrated parsley

3 tbsp Coarsely ground dehydrated sliced limes.

INSTRUCTIONS

Heat oil in a saucepan over medium heat.

Add the garlic and tomatoes and simmer until hot.

Attach chicken, sugar, broth, and raisins and bring to a boil.

Stir in the couscous, cover with a brush.

Take off heat and let sit for 5 minutes.

To taste, add parsley, lime powder, salt, and pepper and shake gently.

Chicken Dumpling Stew

INGREDIENTS

3/4 tsp Rosemary

1/2 tsp Tarragon

1/4 cup Dehydrated chopped scallions or 1/4 cup diced onions Dehydrated chopped celery

1/2 cup Dehydrated cubed potatoes Using 1 cup of dehydrated sliced potatoes.

1/2 cup Dehydrated diced bell pepper Mix of red, green, yellow

1/2 cup Dehydrated carrots

1/2 cup Dehydrated peas

1/2 cup Dehydrated mushrooms

1/4 cup Powdered milk

2/3 cup Flour

4 Chicken breast halves coated

2 large chicken bouillon cubes

2 cups Bisquick or other baking mix Chicken Dumpling Stew

INSTRUCTIONS

In crockpot, mix flour and powdered milk in 10 cups water until I

Remove remaining ingredients, except for the Bisquick.

Place the lid on and cook for 5 1/2 hours at fast.

Mix 2 cups of Bisquick with 1 cup of water in a separate bowl and stir.

Remove the Bisquick mix one heaping tablespoon at a time, about 1/2 hour until you're ready to eat. These will cook in big dumplings with biscuits.

Dehydrated Refried Beans

INGREDIENTS

2 cups Dehydrated refried beans

2 1/2 cups boiling water

1/2 cup Dehydrated chopped green chilies

1 tbsp Dehydrated chopped onion

1/2 tsp Crushed dehydrated sliced jalapeños (optional) Dehydrated Refried Beans

INSTRUCTIONS

To dehydrate refried beans, follow the same procedure as sweet potatoes (see video).

Stir refried dehydrated beans into hot water.

Turn down and blend well.

Add chili peppers, onions, and jalapeños.

Cook for 5 minutes over low heat or until thickened.

Deep Dish Apple Pie

INGREDIENTS

1 tbsp Apple spice

3 tbsp Corn starch

5-6 cups Dehydrated sliced apples

1 cup Sugar

1 whole pie crust Pre-made frozen or home-baked Deep Dish Apple Pie

INSTRUCTIONS

Place dehydrated apples in a wide bowl and fill with adequate boiling water to cover the apples fully.

Let apples sit for 5-10 minutes, then drain water off.

While the apples are still sweet, add the remaining ingredients and mix.

Prepare your pie crust whilst your mixture cools.

Bring the pie together and pour filling in.

Sprinkle over the crust with a little cinnamon and sugar.

Put in preheated oven for 40 minutes at 350 degrees.

Chicken Pot Pie

INGREDIENTS

1/4 cup Dehydrated chopped celery

1/4 cup Dehydrated chopped onion

1 cup Dehydrated cubed potato Or dehydrated sliced potato

1/2 cup Dehydrated peas

1/2 cup Dehydrated sliced carrots

3 whole chicken bouillon cubes

2 cups cooked cubed chicken

2 tbsp Flour

2 whole pre-made pie shells Can make the home as well as

INSTRUCTIONS

Preheat oven to 400 degrees F.

Place all the ingredients in a pot with 6 cups of water and cook until thick at medium heat (about 45 minutes).

Cover the pot and set it until warm for 30 minutes.

Pour the cooked ingredients into a pie shell, then cover with a second pie shell. If not present, cut out slits.

Bake until white, for 40 minutes. Cover the edge of the pie if it starts browning too soon.

Cucumber and Parsley Soup

INGREDIENTS

1 cup Dehydrated sliced cucumbers

1/2 cup green onions Dehydrated 1/4 cup cubed potato chopped scallions Can replace dehydrated green onions.

1/4 cup Dehydrated parsley

1 pinch Rosemary

1/2 tsp Mustard seed

1 big 6.5 cup Chicken bouillon cube Water

INSTRUCTIONS

Dehydrated Cucumbers: place whole cucumbers in boiling water for a couple of minutes to soften.

Cut with a knife or blade made of stainless steel and put on a dehydrator.

Dehydrate for about 10 hours, at 120-125 degrees F.

Preparing Soup: In a pot with 6 1/2 cups of boiling water, add all ingredients and put the lid on.

Bring the soup to a rolling boil and then rising to medium heat and cook for 30 minutes.

Chicken Salad Sandwich

INGREDIENTS

15 oz cans chicken chunks

1/2 cup mayonnaise

2 tbsp Dehydrated chopped celery

1 tsp Chopped onion

2 cups Dehydrated bean sprouts

INSTRUCTIONS

Mix all ingredients together.

Let set on sandwiches for 15-20 minutes before spreading out.

Assemble and enjoy sandwiches.

Chocolate Walnut Brownies

INGREDITIONS

4 oz. Chopped unsweetened chocolate

1/2 cup butter flavored shortening

2 cups Sugar

2 tsp Vanilla extract

4 tbsp Powdered whole eggs

1 cup Flour White or whole wheat

1 cup Chopped walnuts May cover pecans

4 tbsp Chocolate

INSTRUCTIONS

In a pot placed on the stove, over very low heat, melt chocolate and shorten, stirring continuously until smooth. Fully Good.

Preheat oven to 350 ° C.

Add the sugar and vanilla, then stir well until mixed.

The powdered eggs and 4 Tbsp water are combined in a separate small bowl.

Attach the egg mixture to the pot, and start stirring.

Add the flour and nuts to the saucepan and stir until mixed.

Pour the batter into an 8x8 inch grated pan.

Bake for 25 minutes, or clean until a toothpick comes out. Then cut fully into squares to cool.

Cranberry Sauce

INGREDIENTS

1/2 cup Dehydrated cranberries

1 1/2 cup Water

3/4 cup Sugar Cranberry Sauce

INSTRUCTIONS

Set ingredients into a sauce pan.

Bring to a rolling boil for around 30 minutes to reduce and thicken on a high, then lower temperature to medium.

Before serving, allow to cool and chill.

Corn Bread

INGREDIENTS

2 cups Dehydrated cubed potato

1 cup Dehydrated corn

1/3 cup Dehydrated chopped onion

1/3 cup Dehydrated peas

1/3 cup Dehydrated carrots whole baby, or sliced

2 tbsp Powdered butter (Mix with 1 tbsp warm water).

Can substitute fresh butter.

1 tsp Black pepper

2 whole chicken bouillon cubes or 3-4 tbsp bouillon powder

2 tsp Garlic powder

1 cup Powdered milk

2 tbsp Corn starch

12 cups Water

INSTRUCTIONS

In a large pot, bring 12 cups of water to boil.

Add dehydrated vegetables, butter, spices, and bullion to the pot.

Stir and reduce heat to simmer, then cook until vegetables are tender, about 1 hour.

In a separate bowl, put in the powdered milk and corn starch, add 2 cups of warm water and whisk to blend well.

Add milk mixture to the soup pot, stir to blend well.

Turn flame to medium-low, stirring constantly. When soup begins to boil, reduce to simmer and stir until liquid begins to thicken slightly.

Variations: If you happen to have a few small cans of chopped clams, you can throw that in. Or, you can add ham bone, chunks of leftover ham, fried bacon pieces, or Spam.

Corn Chowder

INGREDIENTS

2 cups Dehydrated cubed potato

1 cup Dehydrated maize

1/3 cup Dehydrated chopped onion

1/3 cup Dehydrated peas

1/3 cup Dehydrated carrots whole baby, or sliced

2 tbsp Powdered butter (mixed with 1 tsp warm water). May take the place of fresh butter.

1 tsp Black pepper

2 whole chicken bouillon cubes or 3-4 tbsp bouillon powder

2 tsp Garlic powder

1 cup Condensed milk

2 tbsp Corn starch

12 cups Water

INSTRUCTIONS

Bring 12 cups of water to a boil in a big pot.

Fill the bowl with dehydrated vegetables, butter, spices, and bullion.

Remove and rising heat to boiling, then cook for around 1 hour, until vegetables are tender.

Put in the powdered milk and maize starch in a separate pot, add 2 cups of warm water and whisk to mix properly.

Add milk to the soup pot and whisk to mix properly.

Switch the flame to medium-low, continuously stirring. When the soup begins boiling, reduce to simmer and stir until the liquid begins thickening slightly.

Variations: You can add that in if you happen to have a few tiny cans of chopped clams. Or, you can add ham bone, leftover ham chunks, fried bacon bits, or spam.

Made in the USA
Monee, IL
13 May 2020

30959911R00095